Art
Companion

by
Gary Llama

OVOLR! / DEBACKLE
Richmond, Virginia

ART COMPANION, by Gary Llama

© *Copyright 2017, Gary Llama*

Published by
OVOLR! / DEBACKLE
Richmond, Virginia

ISBN: 978-0-9986977-3-4

WORKS

2009 - 2015

A Catalog Of Life Processes

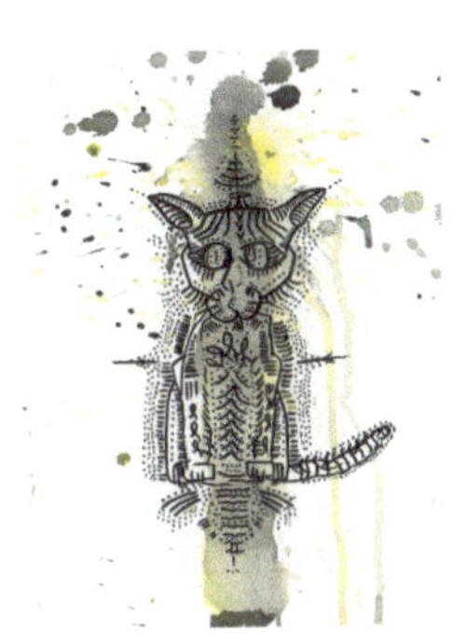

fig 1.
Acrylic on Paper.
8.5 x 11".
2009

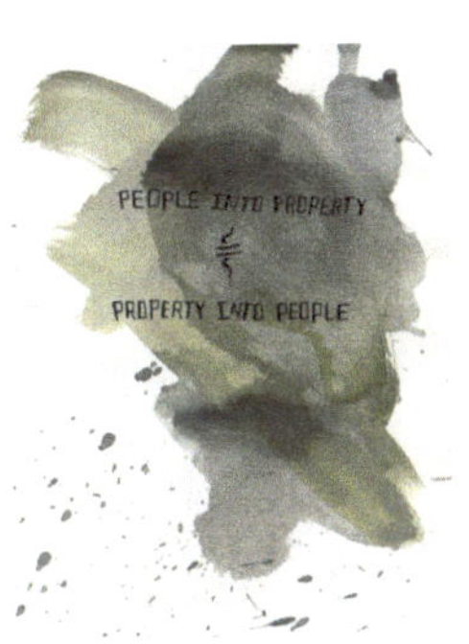

fig 2.
Acrylic on Paper.
8.5 x 11".
2009

fig 3.
Acrylic on Paper.
8.5 x 11".
2009

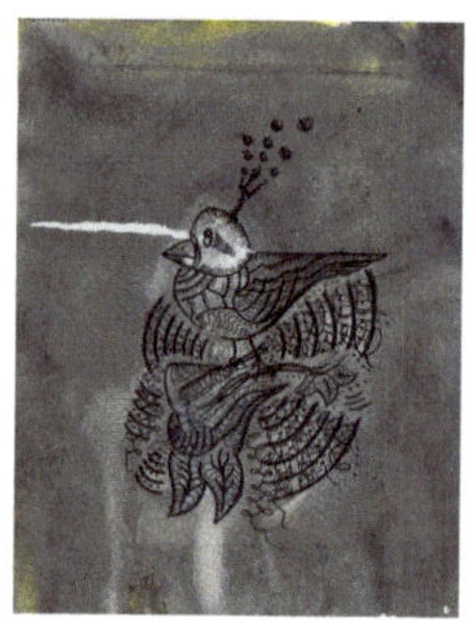

fig 4.
Acrylic on Paper.
8.5 x 11".
2009

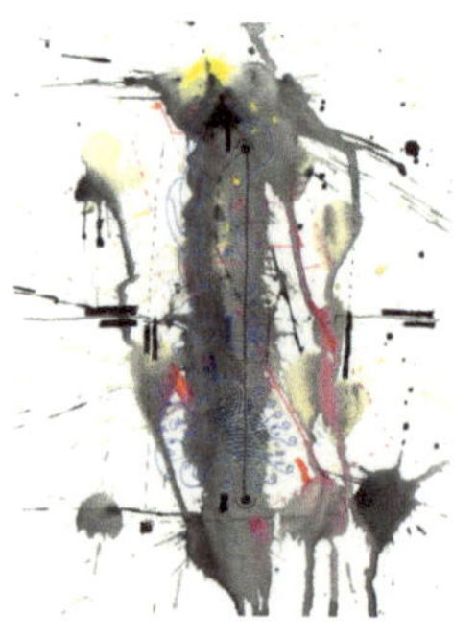

An Anatomie

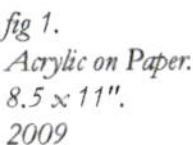

fig 1.
Acrylic on Paper.
8.5 x 11".
2009

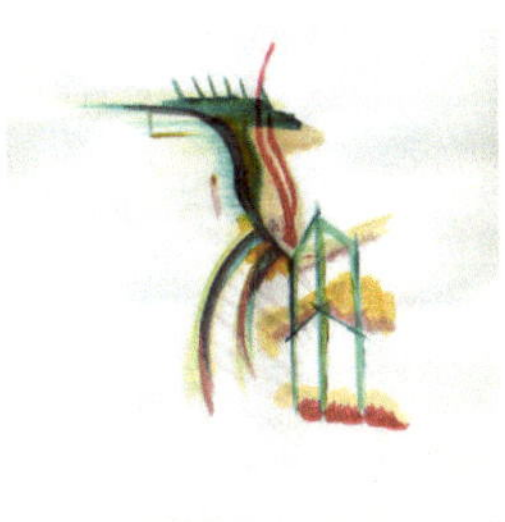

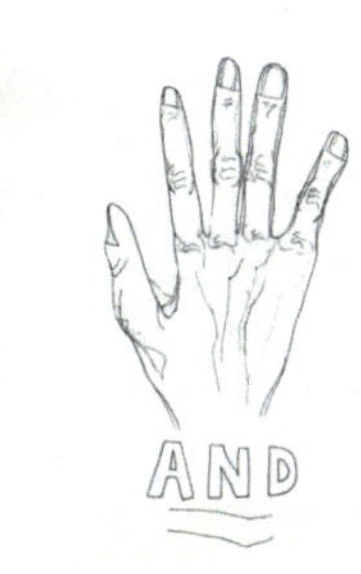

fig 2.
Acrylic on Paper.
8.5 x 11".
2009

fig 3.
Acrylic on Paper.
8.5 x 11".
2010

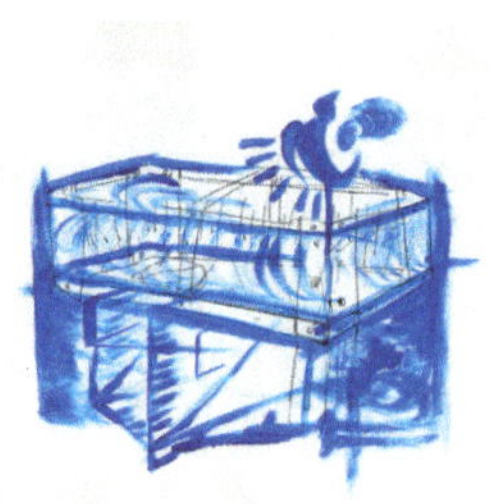

fig 4.
Acrylic on Paper.
8.5 x 11".
2010

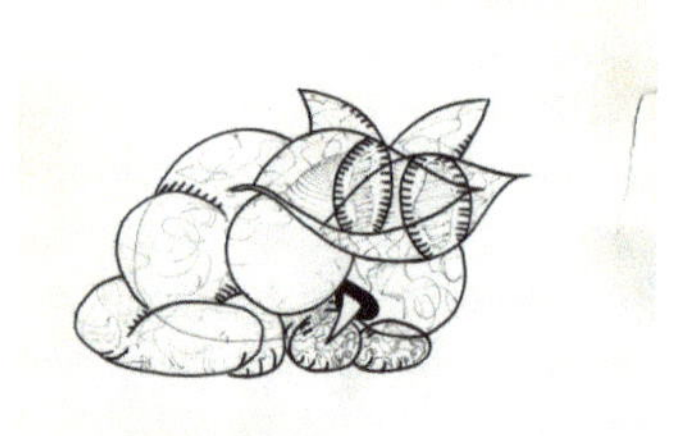

Eat The Fat

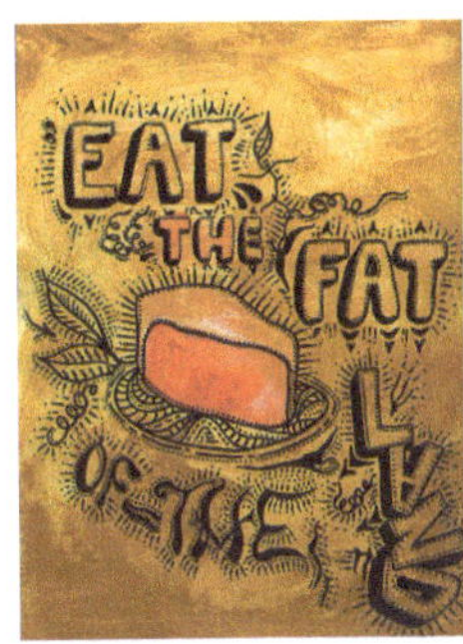

fig 1.
Acrylic on Paper.
8.5 x 11".
2009

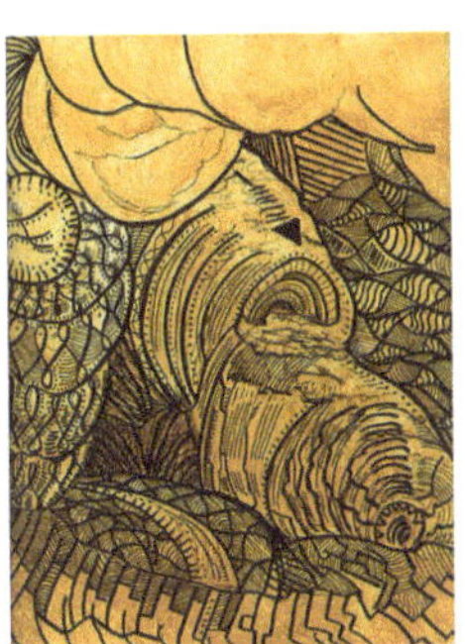

fig 2.
Acrylic on Paper.
8.5 x 11".
2009

fig 3.
Acrylic on Paper.
8.5 x 11".
2009

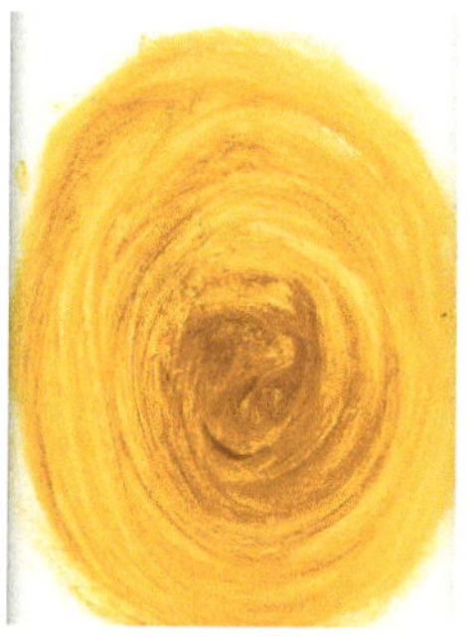

fig 4.
Acrylic on Paper.
8.5 x 11".
2009

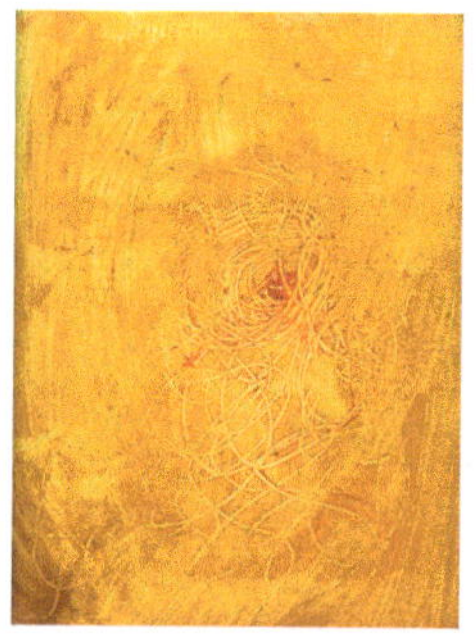

Mini-Bontecou

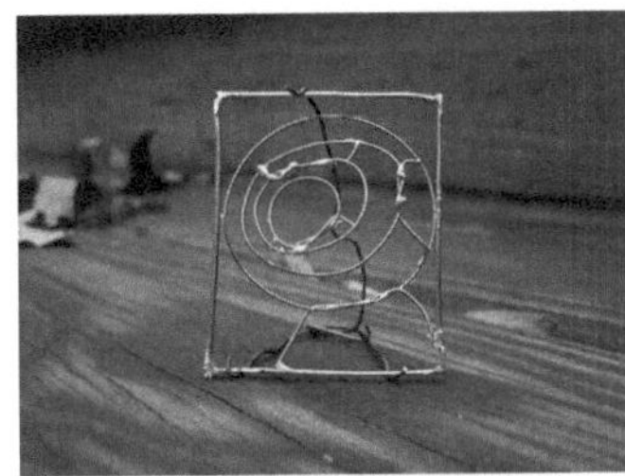

*fig 1.
Wire, guitar string,
paper clips, solder
2.25" × 3.4"
2009*

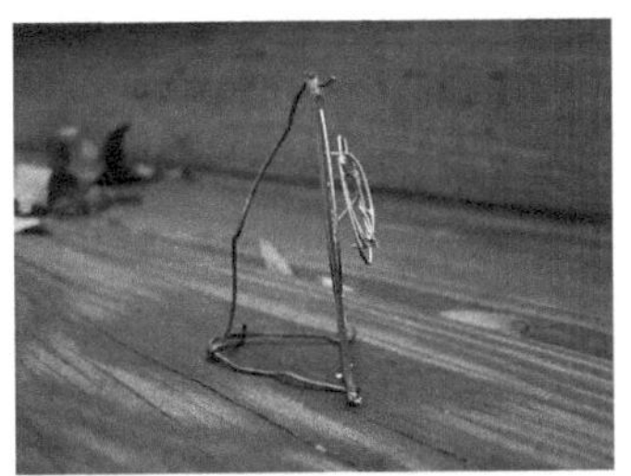

Danger System

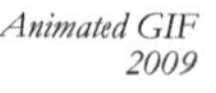

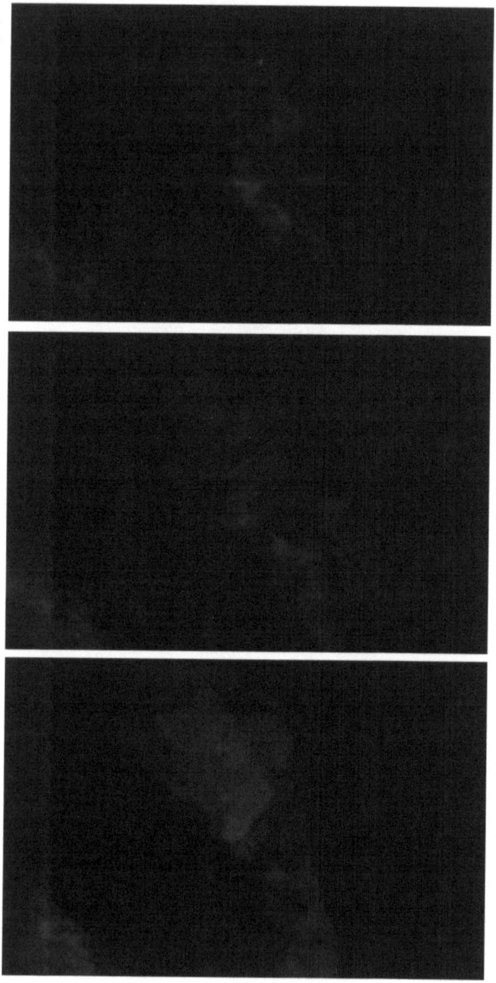

You Did The Right Thing

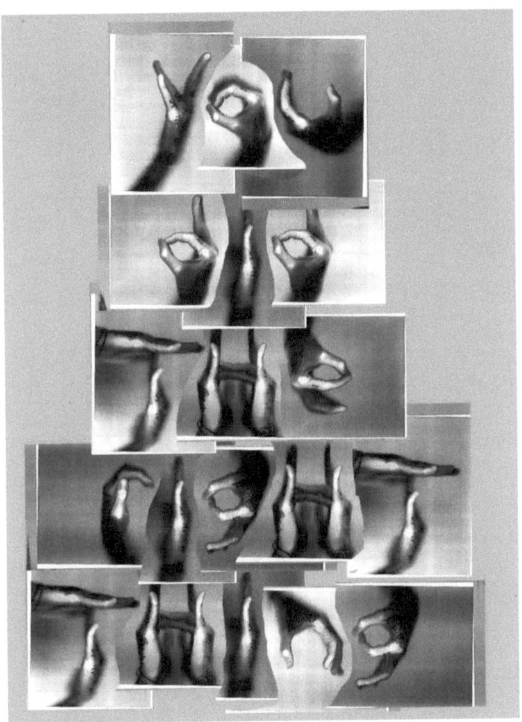

Self doubt can be horrible. I noticed the tendency in myself, and in my friends, and took note of the sometimes continuing conflict one can cope with internally. Mostly because rarely do we get reassurance in decisions.

So, in 2009 I decided I wanted to make a treat, to confirm when people did a good thing.

I made this graphic on a scanner.

Then I bought the domain, 'youdidtherightthing.com'.

Then when friends had doubt, I texted the URL to them.

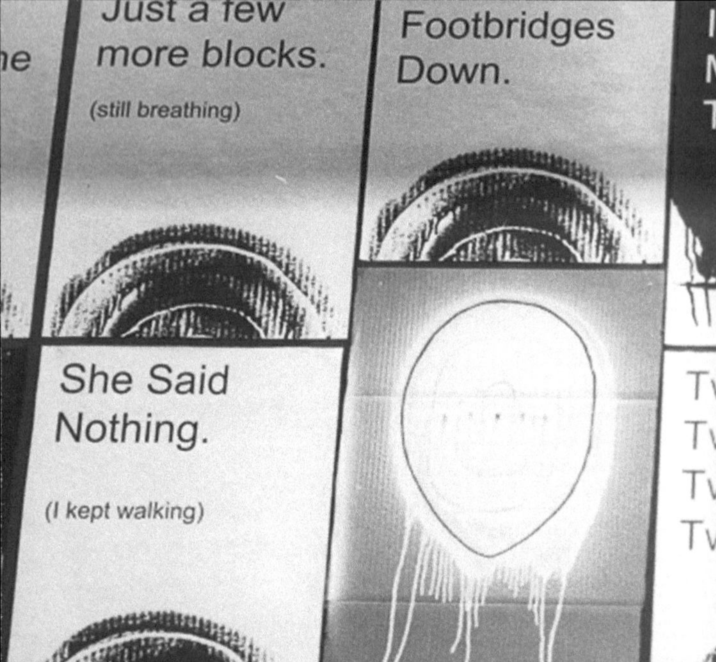

An Identity Of The Pedestrian In The City

March 2011.
Crossroads Coffee & Ice Cream
Richmond, Virginia

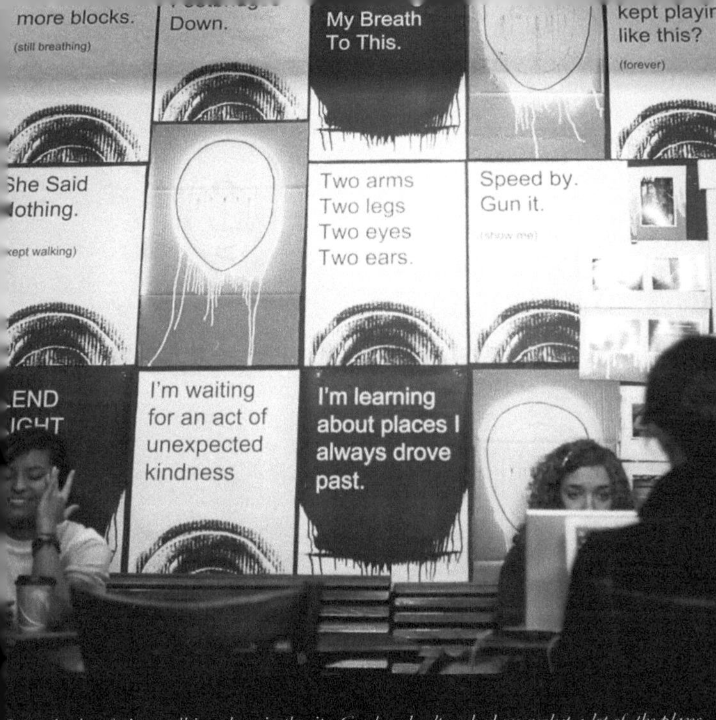

I spend a lot of time walking places in the city. Car-based culture had me neglect a lot of the places I've been. The small details. Cities are full of them. Marks and indentions in place that serve as historical record. Moving through this environment in the car reduces it's signifigance to a blur: It encourages the traveller to take the place for granted rather easily.

In the west, and especially in cities where public transit doesn not really exist, and most travel is by car, Walking is a degraded act. The pedestrian is prejudiced with a variety of statuses: Poor, Homeless, Student, Troublemaker. And at every light, the pedestrian competes for right-of-way with the car. To have something so different than you, a machine mostly made of steel and plastic, as the partner in travelling, against your comparatively crushable bone and flesh, makes interaction one of constant vigilance.

To me though, walking can be a meditative experience: Think your thoughts, make your breath, feel your feet settling onto and off of the pavement. You think of where you are going. You think of where you are coming from. You think of nothing. You decompress. You prepare. Walking across an urban situation has a multiplicty of emotions and uses..

Photograph of show wall by Kieran Wagner

fig 1.
Aerosol on
Cardboard.
8.5 x 14"
(Approx)
2011

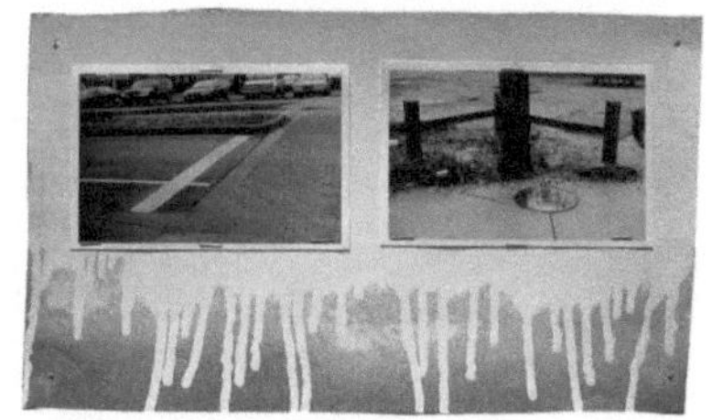

fig 2.
Aerosol on
Cardboard.
8.5 x 14"
(Approx)
2011

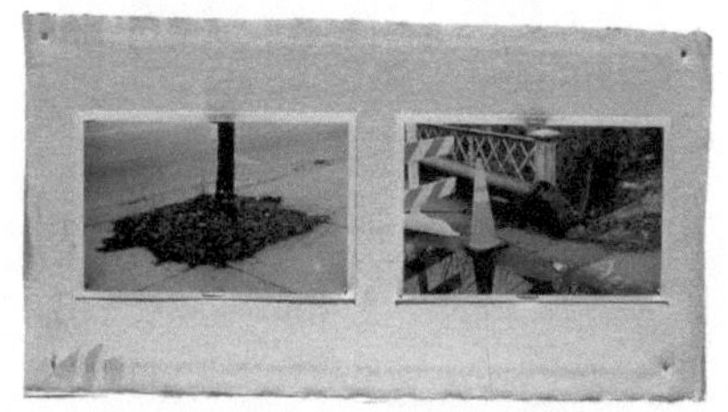

fig 3.
Aerosol on Cardboard.
8.5 x 14" (Approx)
2011

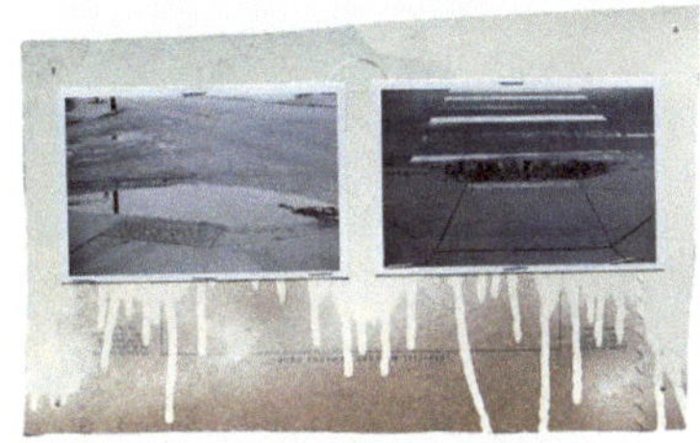

fig 4.
Aerosol on Cardboard.
8.5 x 14" (Approx)
2011

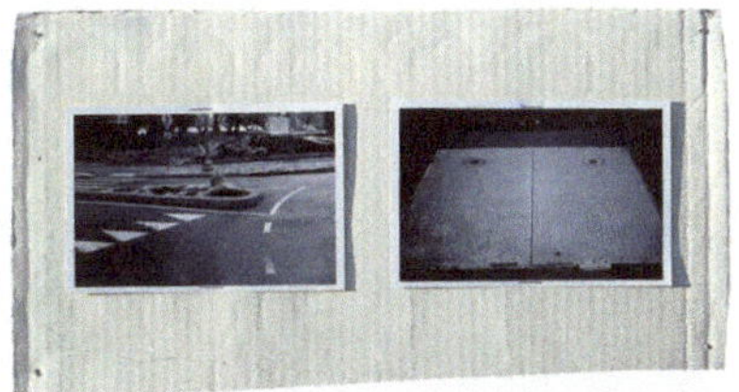

fig 5.
Aerosol on
Cardboard.
8.5 x 14"
(Approx)
2011

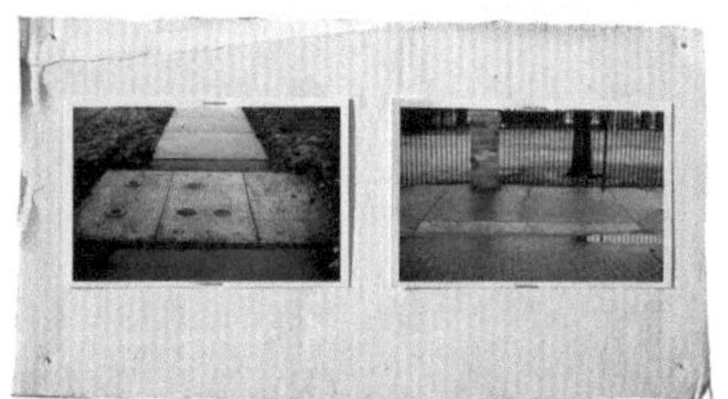

fig 6.
Aerosol on
Cardboard.
8.5 x 14"
(Approx)
2011

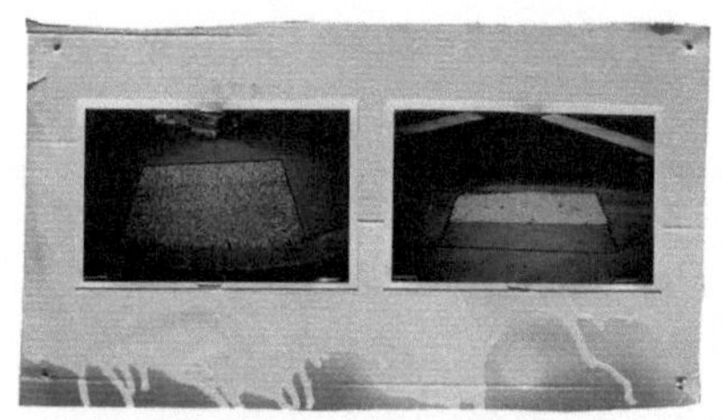

fig 7.
Aerosol on Cardboard.
8.5 x 14" (Approx)
2011

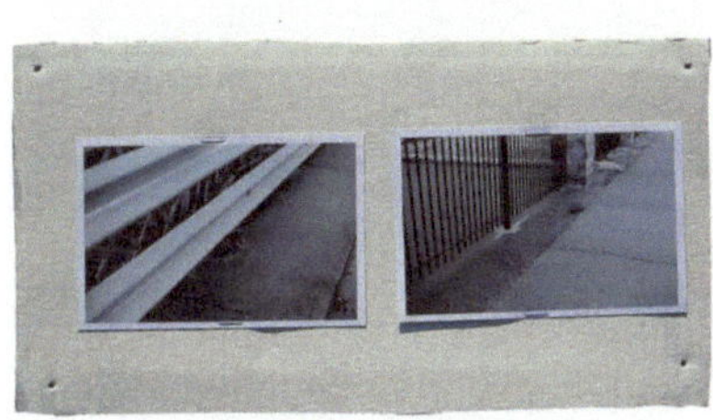

fig 8.
Aerosol on Cardboard.
5.5 x 8" (Approx)
2011

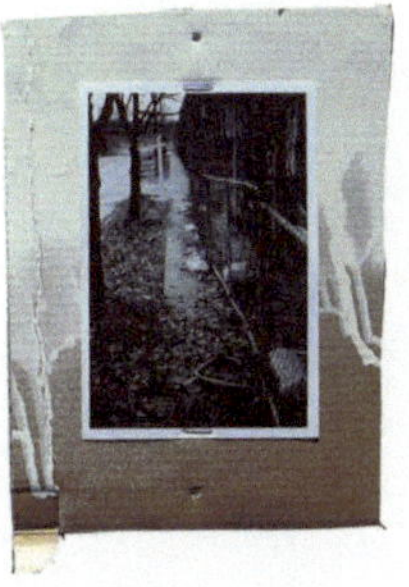

fig 1.
Thermal print on
paper.
18 x 24"
(Approx)
2011

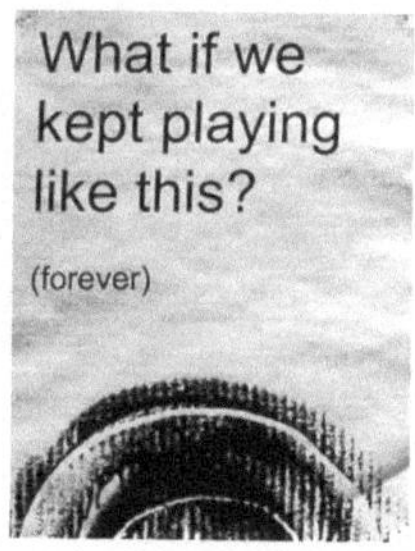

fig 2.
Thermal print on
paper.
18 x 24"
(Approx)
2011

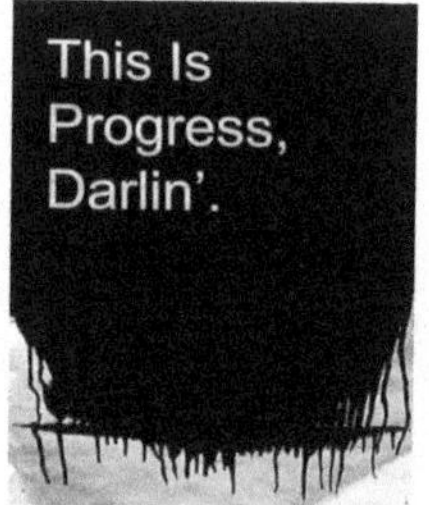

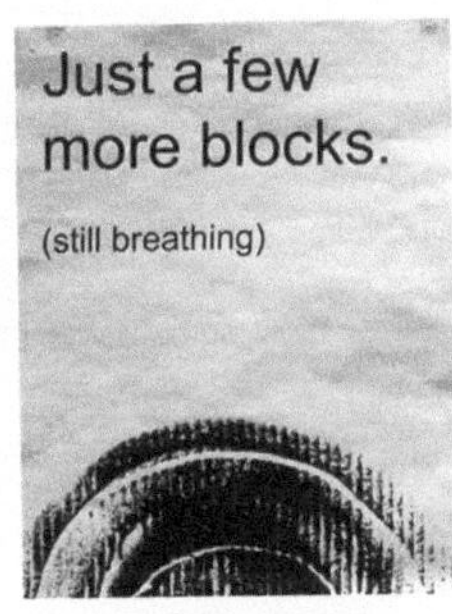

fig 3.
Thermal print on paper.
18 x 24" (Approx)
2011

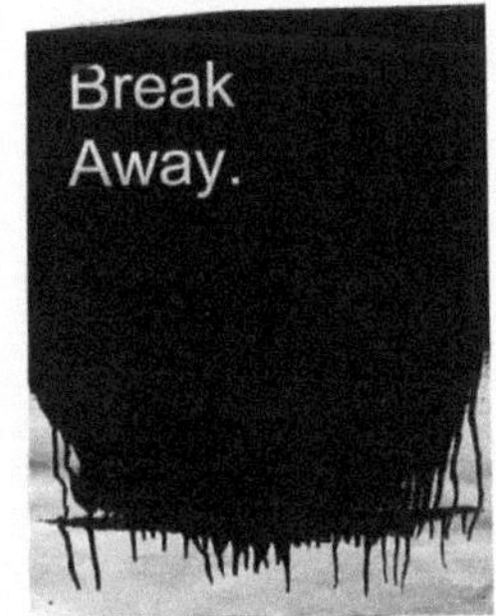

fig 4.
Thermal print on paper.
18 x 24" (Approx)
2011

fig 5.
Thermal print on
paper.
18 x 24"
(Approx)
2011

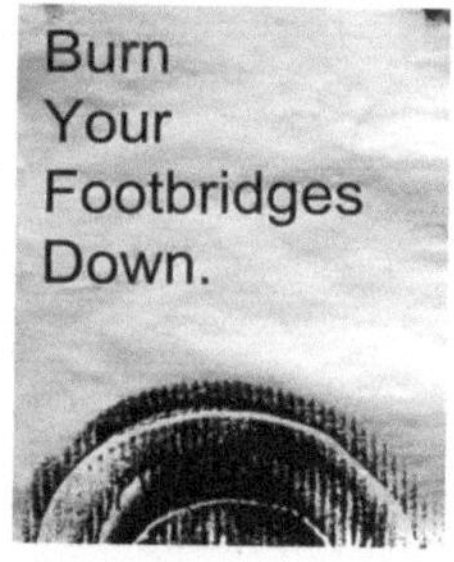
Burn
Your
Footbridges
Down.

fig 6.
Thermal print on
paper.
18 x 24"
(Approx)
2011

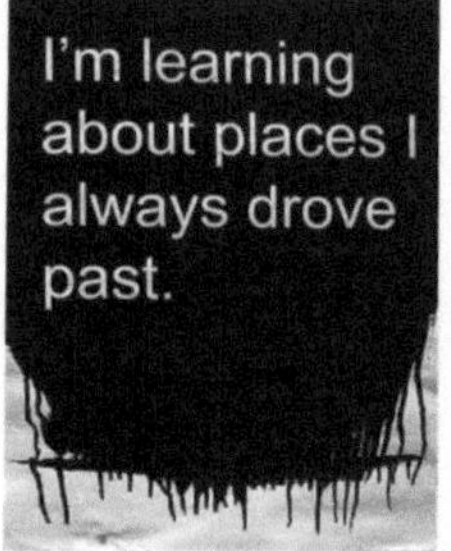
I'm learning
about places I
always drove
past.

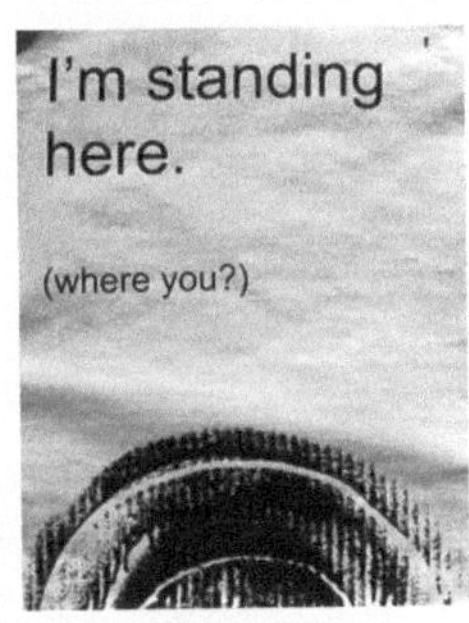

fig 7.
Thermal print on
paper.
18 x 24" (Approx)
2011

fig 8.
Thermal print on
paper.
18 x 24" (Approx)
2011

fig 9.
Thermal print on
paper.
18 x 24"
(Approx)
2011

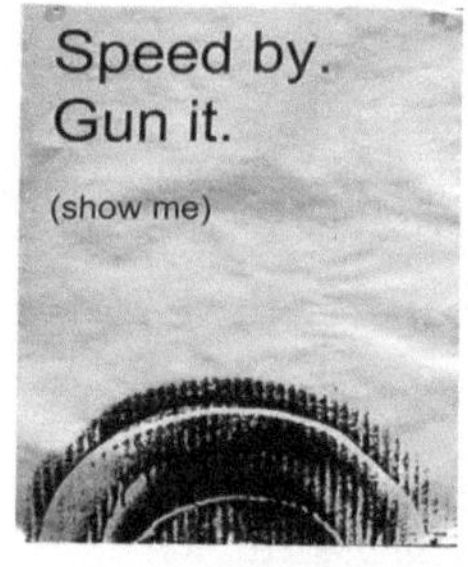

fig 10.
Thermal print on
paper.
18 x 24"
(Approx)
2011

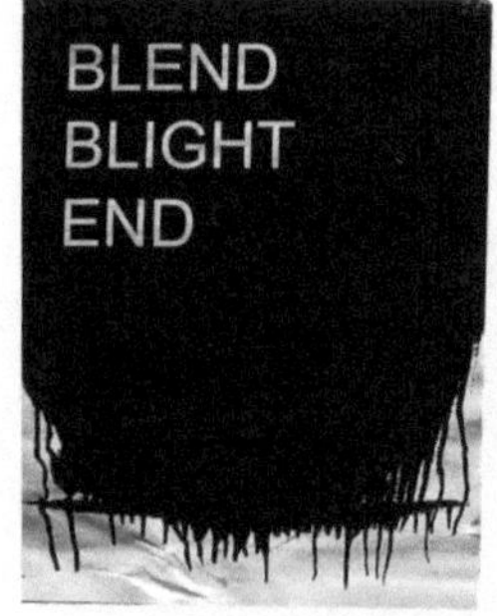

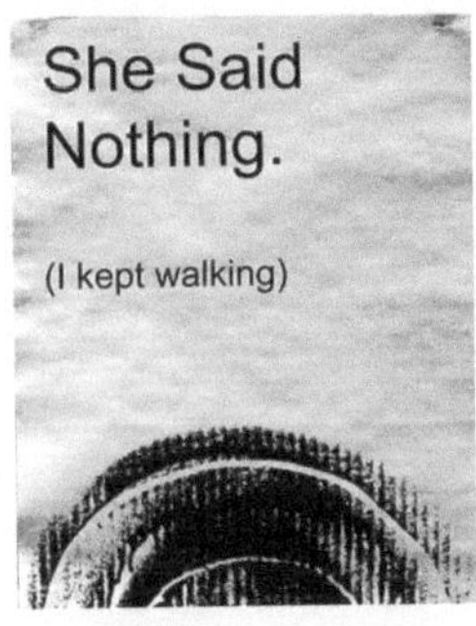

fig 11.
Thermal print on paper.
18 x 24" (Approx)
2011

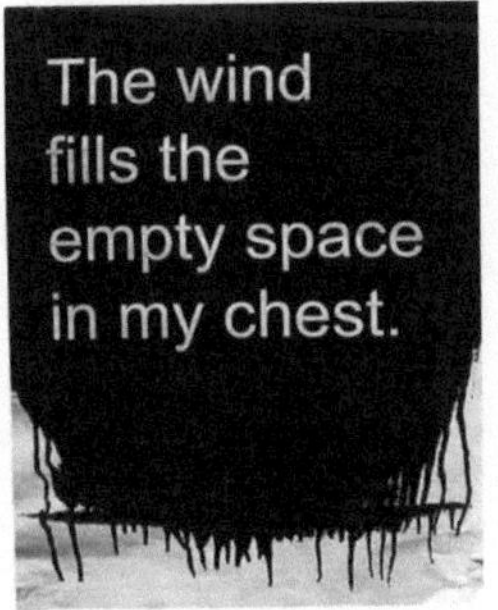

fig 12.
Thermal print on paper.
18 x 24" (Approx)
2011

fig 13.
Thermal print on
paper.
18 x 24"
(Approx)
2011

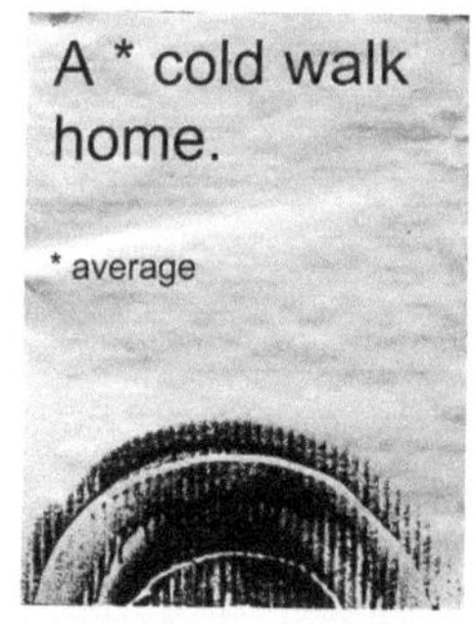

fig 14.
Thermal print on
paper.
18 x 24"
(Approx)
2011

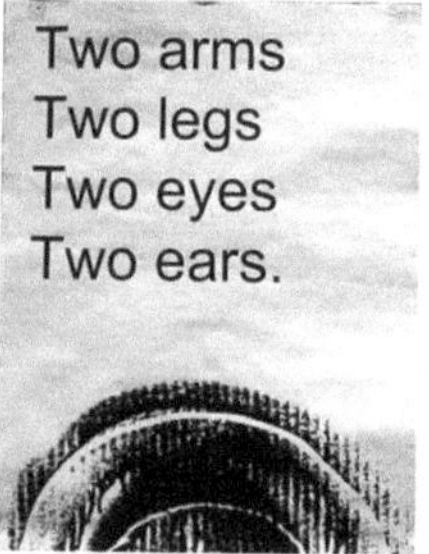

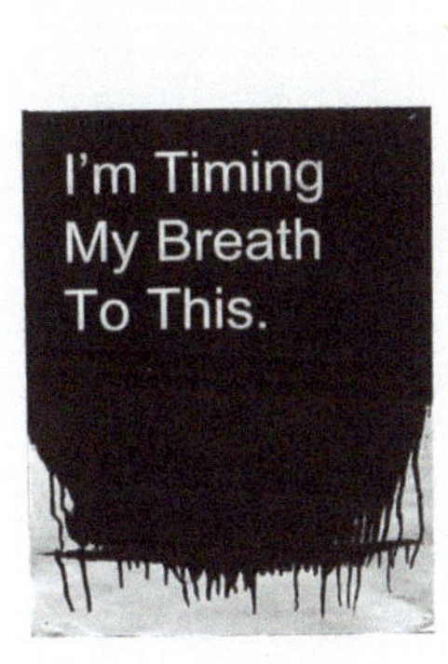

fig 15.
Thermal print on
paper.
18 x 24" (Approx)
2011

fig 16.
Thermal print on
paper.
18 x 24" (Approx)
2011

fig 17.
Thermal print on
paper.
18 x 24"
(Approx)
2011

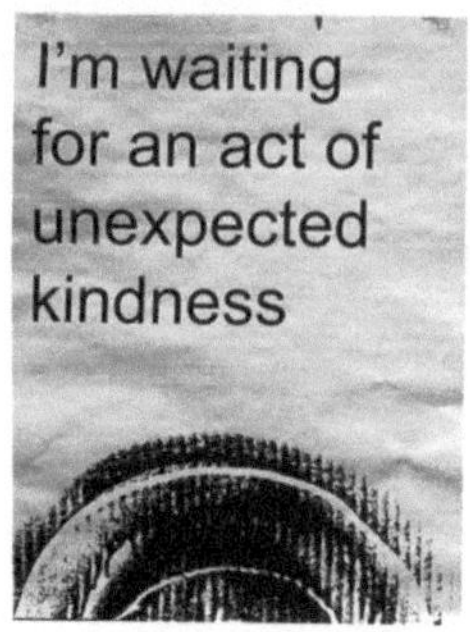

I'm waiting
for an act of
unexpected
kindness

fig 18.
Thermal print on
paper.
18 x 24"
(Approx)
2011

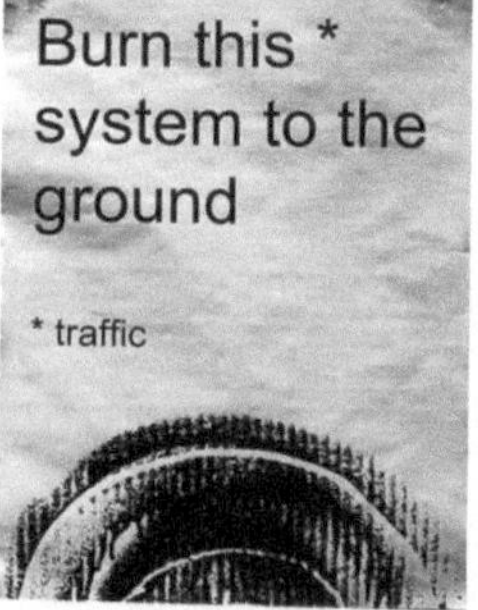

Burn this *
system to the
ground

* traffic

Pedestrian Targets

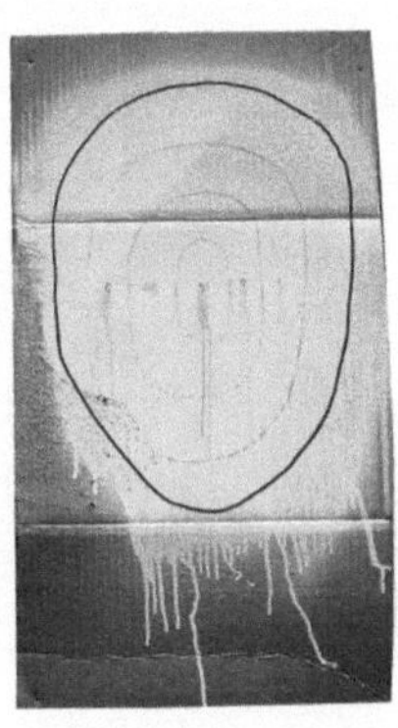

fig 1.
Acrylic on Cardboard.
18 x 29" (Approx)
2011

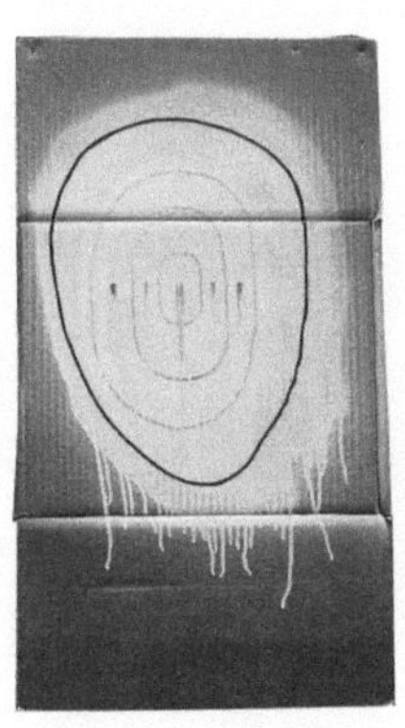

fig 2.
Acrylic on Cardboard.
18 x 29" (Approx)
2011

fig 3.
Acrylic on
Cardboard.
18 x 29"
(Approx)
2011

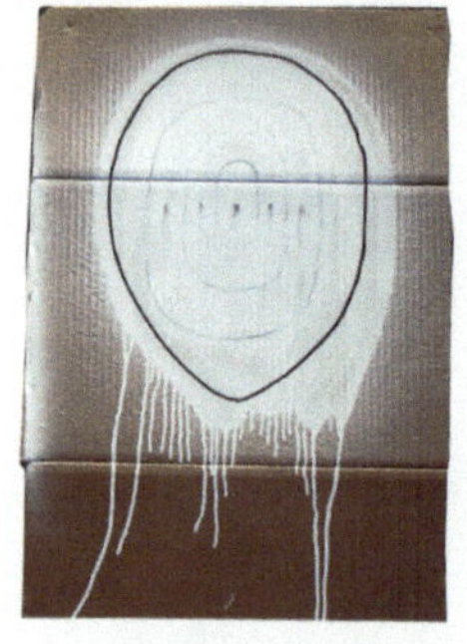

fig 4.
Acrylic on
Cardboard.
18 x 29"
(Approx)
2011

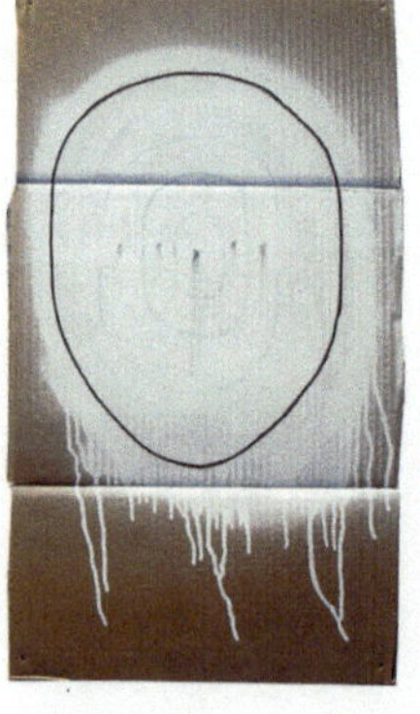

Marker

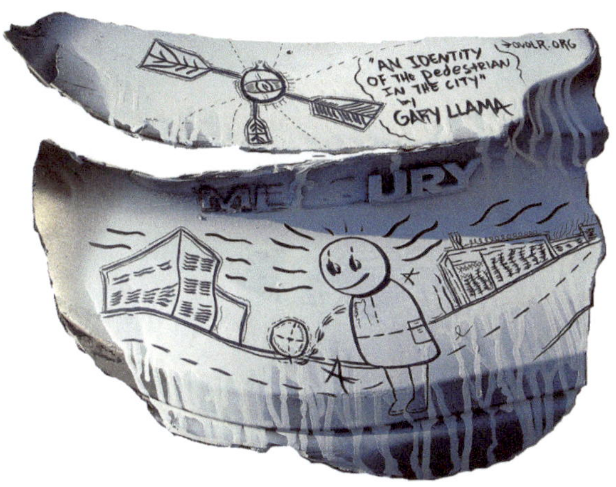

Acrylic, marker on plastic found object.
12 x 18" (Approx)
2011

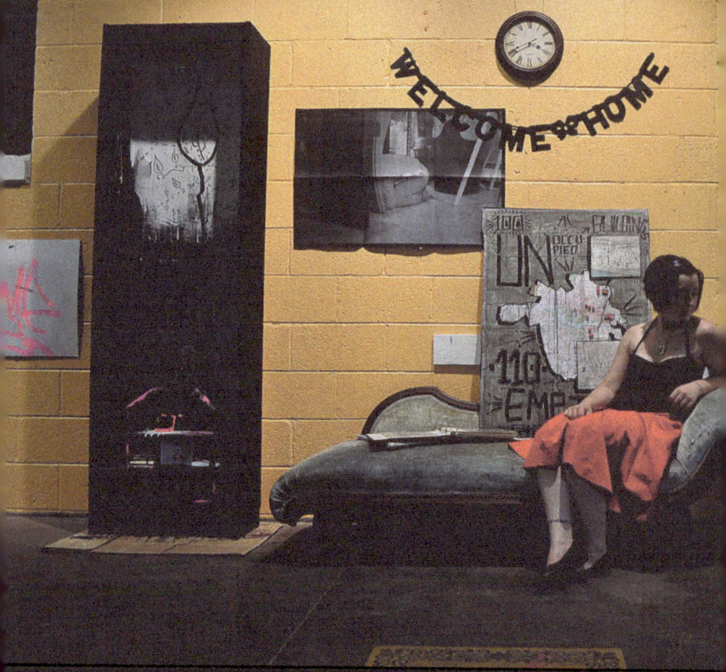

Home: An Exploration

May 2011.
OneTribe Organics
Richmond, Virginia

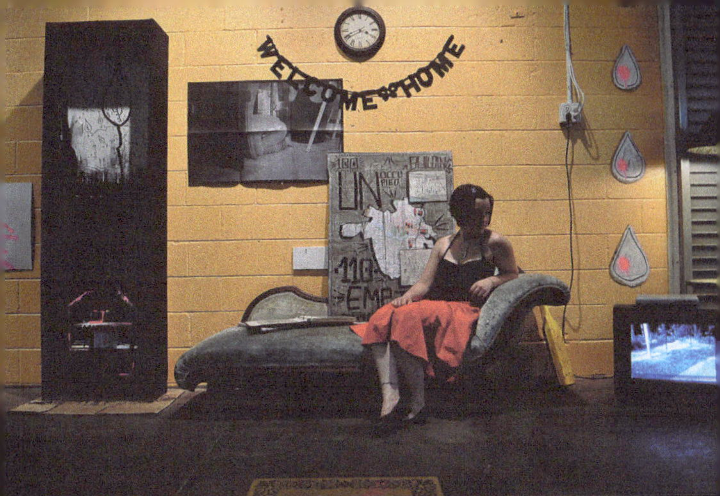

The Home show was a collaborative work between Me and my spouse, Megan Osborn. When we first approached the show, our idea was to highlight the large amount of unoccupied buildings in Richmond. These could be abandoned, condemened, for sale, for rent: As long as no one was in them, legally.

We set out to catalog these buildings, photographing them in the style of a scientist: same framing, head-on, no art to it at all. We chose to find one hundred of these buildings. We had no idea what the difficulty of this would be, we just trusted we would find them.

We began picking neighborhoods we knew, and moved on to ones we did not. As we photographed the houses, Megan recorded their addresses. About two days in, she purchased a map of the city. We used the map to find new neighborhoods, and by the time the show would open, she had accurately plotted all their positions with pushpins. We spent many a spring day walking across Richmond, cameras and clipboard in hand.

In the living room sat a book with the photographs of over 110 unoccupied dwellings, with a map holding pushpins at various locations in the city of Richmond, places people used to call home. In the process of building the show, the artists visited and photographed these buildings, marking their address on a map. The locations were chosen at random and carried out of the course of a few weeks.

Also, included was a cabinent recalling communication. As people become more transient, the idea of Home may become something of a mindset, ala Non-Places.

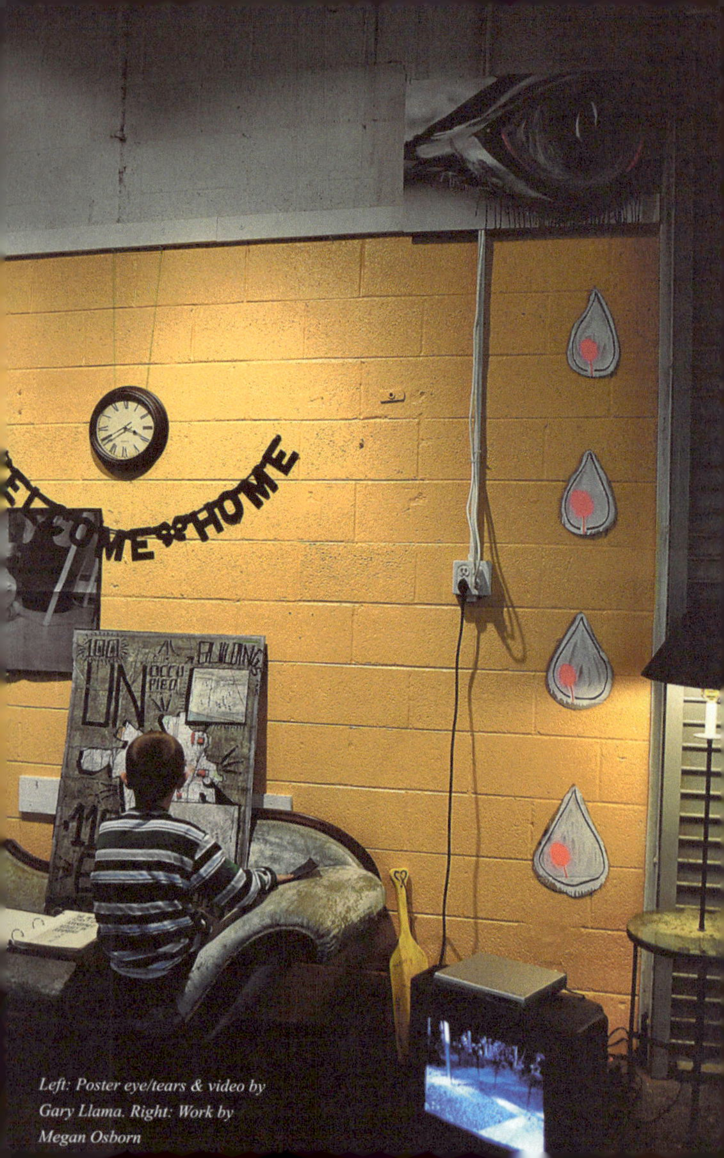

Left: Poster eye/tears & video by Gary Llama. Right: Work by Megan Osborn

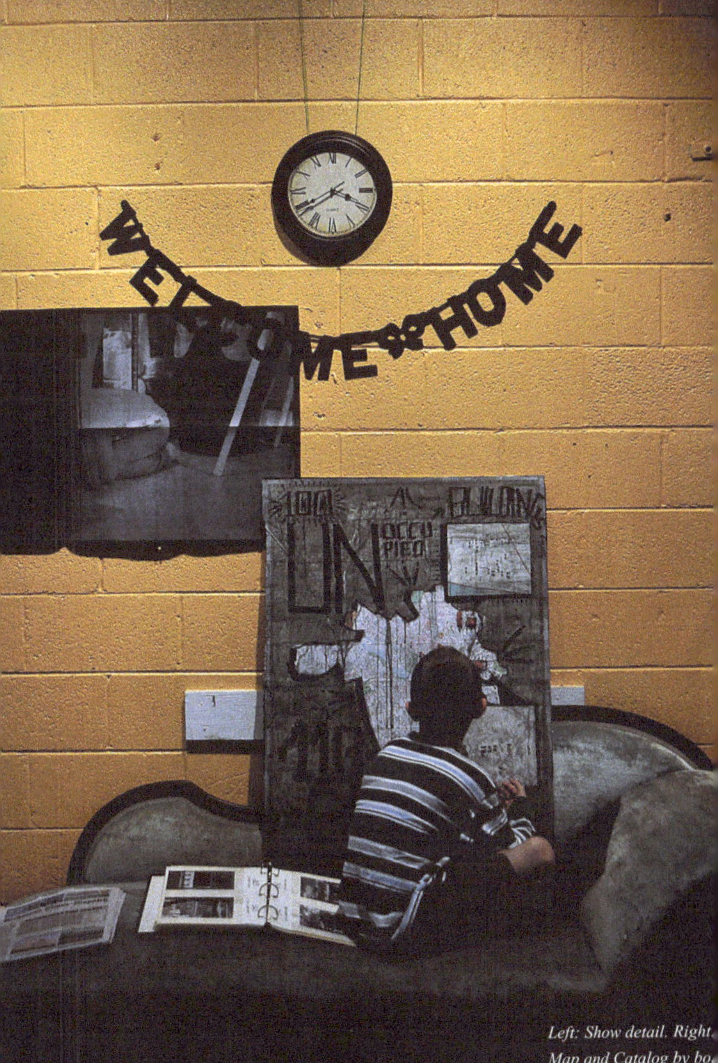

Left: Show detail. Right
Map and Catalog by bo
artists.

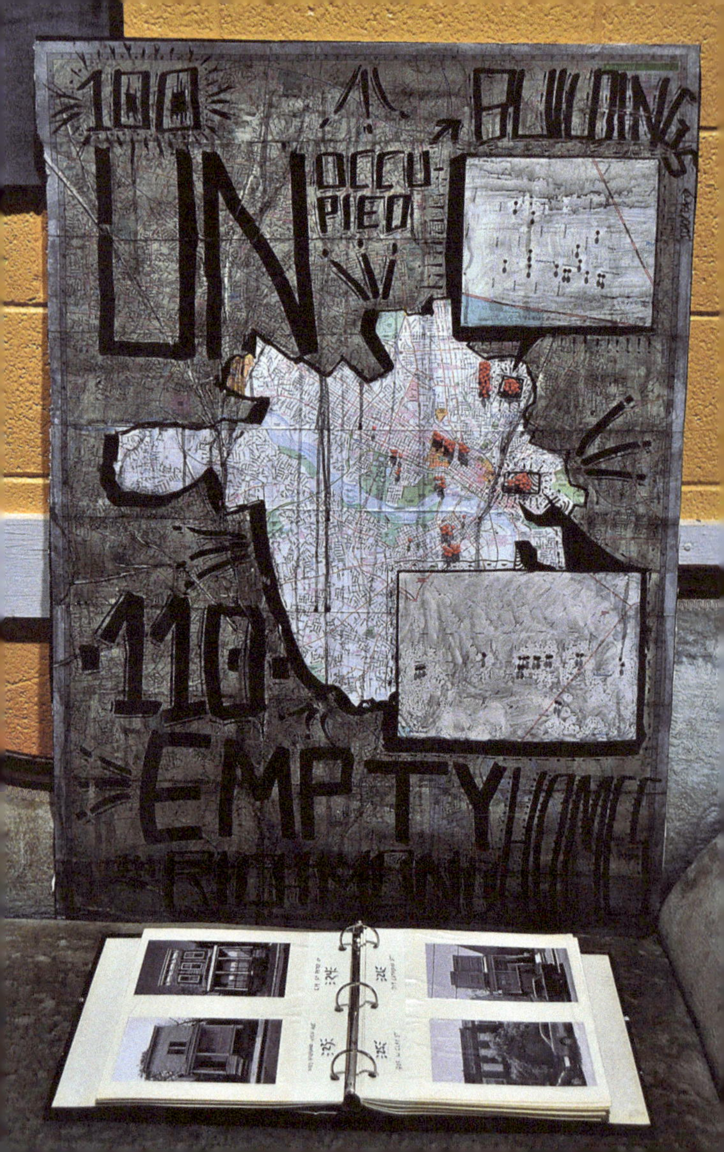

100
UN OCCU- PIED BUILDINGS
110
EMPTY

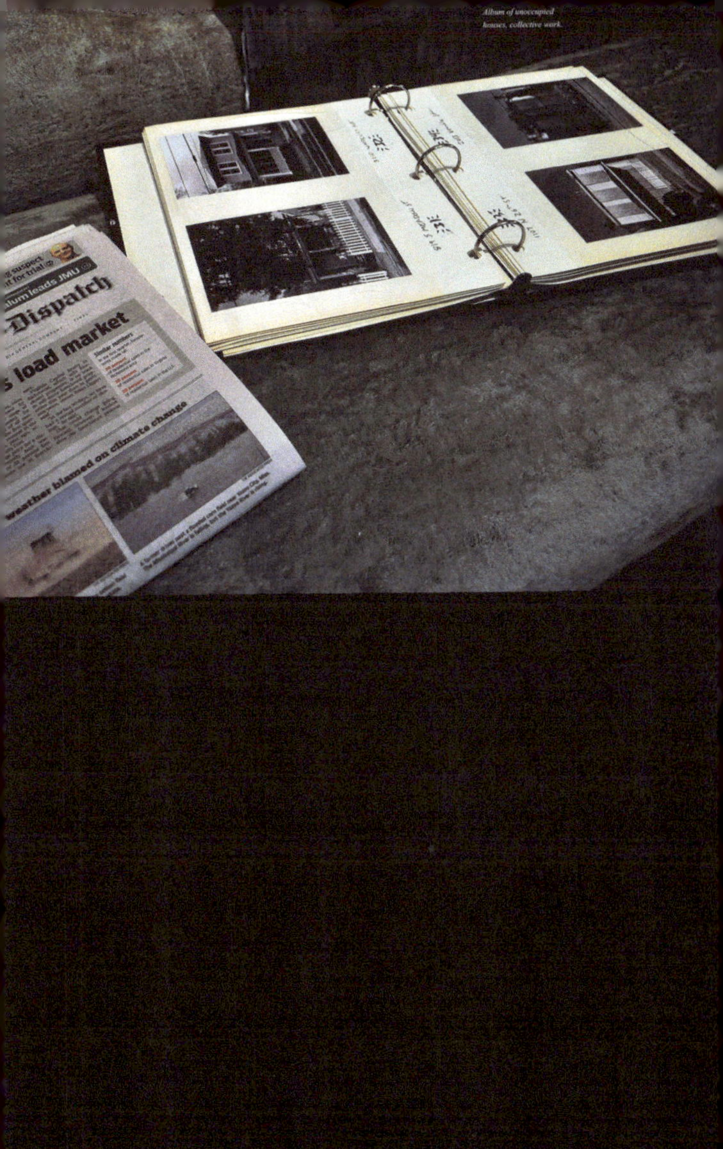

Album of unoccupied houses, collective work.

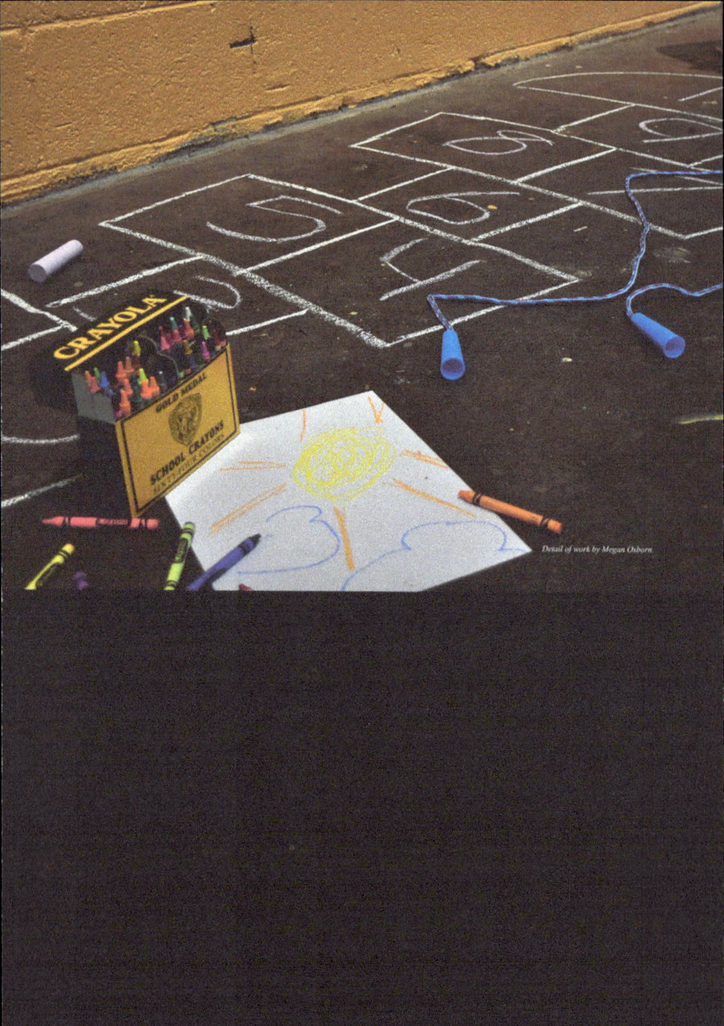

Detail of work by Megan Osborn

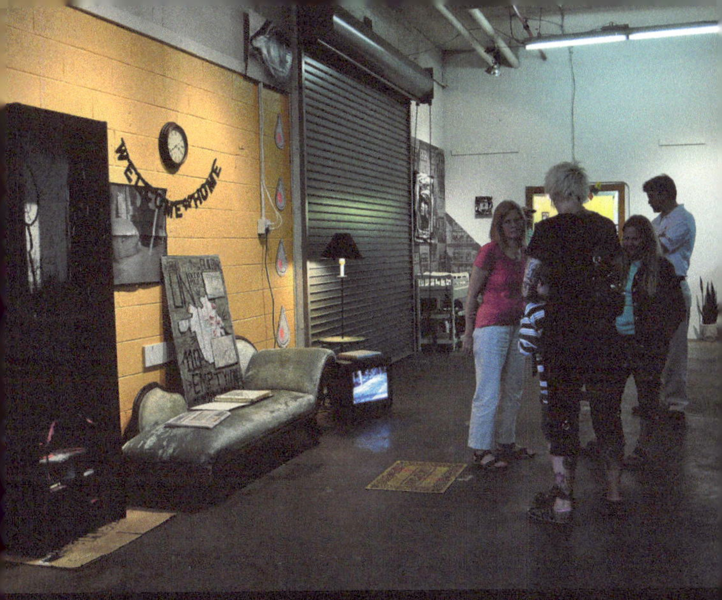

Photos of show by M. Osborn.
First image of show by Gary Llama.

Pieces 'Home: An Exploration'

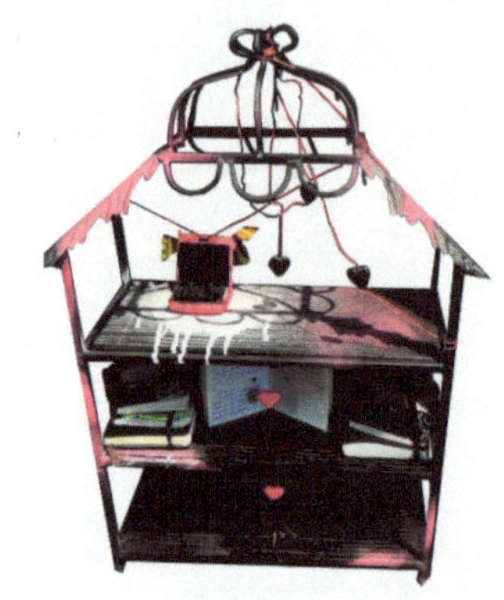

Birdcage.
Acrylic, mixed
media on steel.
21 x 32" x 8"
(Approx)
2011

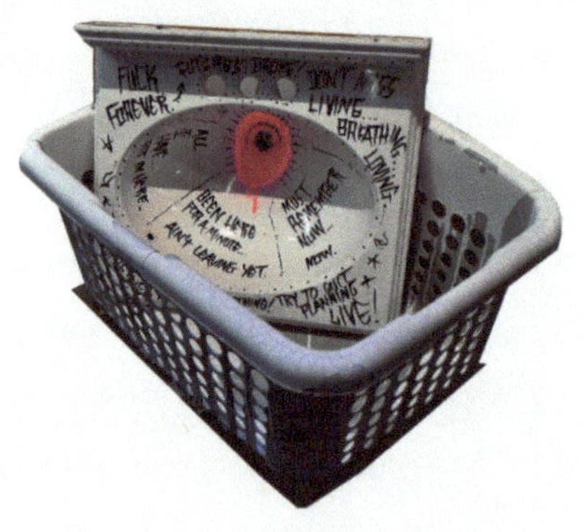

Kitchen Sink.
Acrylic on laundry
basket, sink.
18 x 34" x 18"
(Approx)
2011

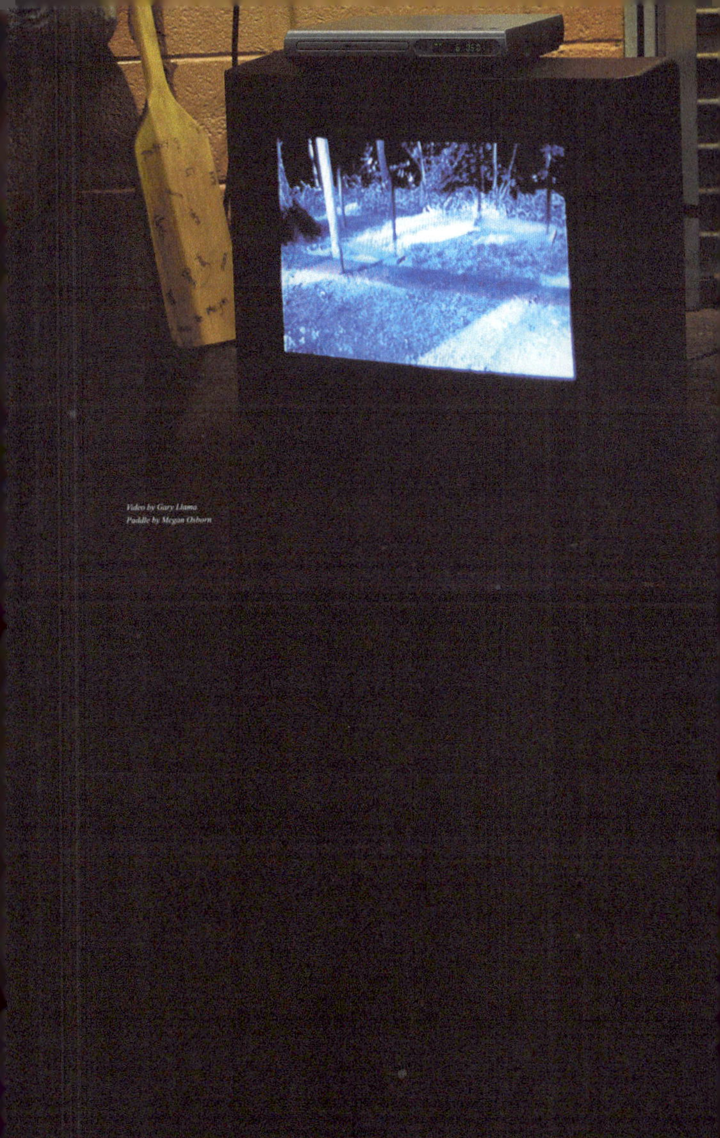

Video by Gary Llama
Paddle by Megan Osborn

millions
A B C D
F G H I J
K L M N

Millions

February-April 2012.
Crossroads Coffee & Ice Cream
Richmond, Virginia

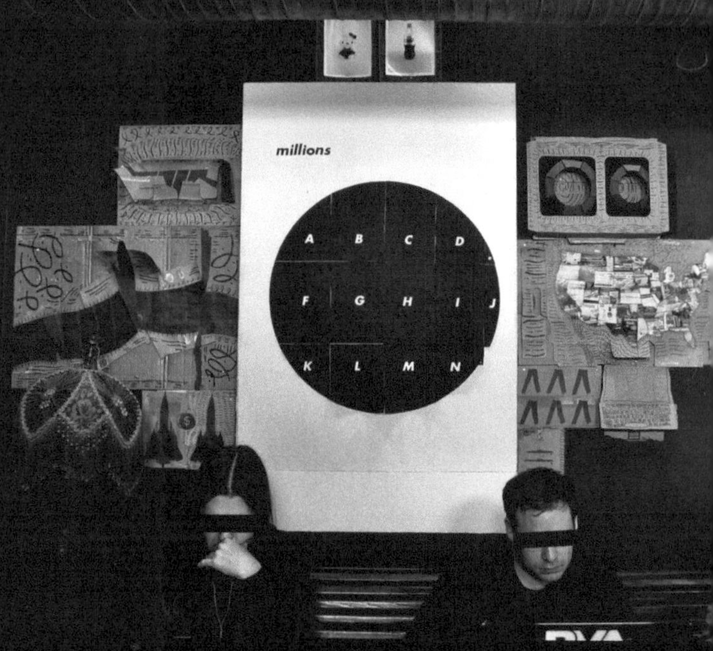

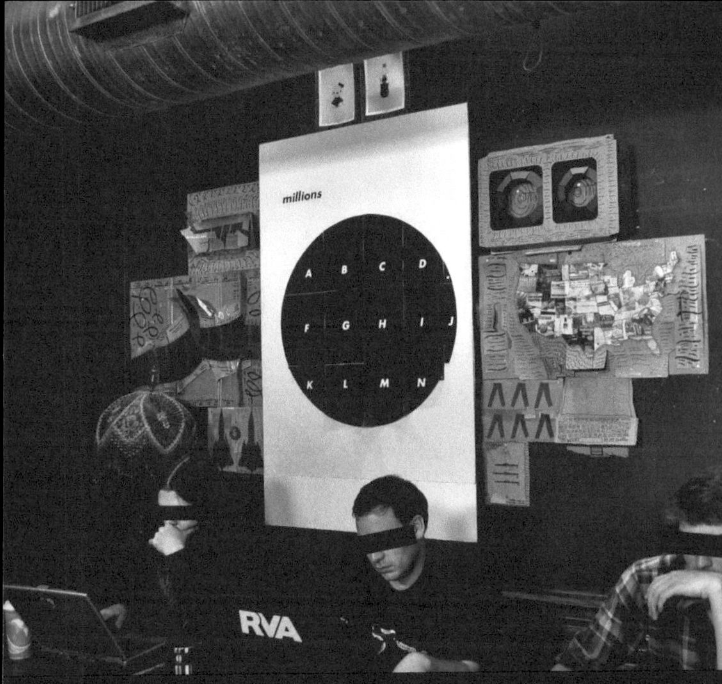

We cannot relate to huge numbers.

We cannot fathom our uniformity.

And we tend to view atrocity as accident.

When we realize our uniformity is the result of mass marketed solutions...

When we realize atrocity is a calcualated risk of our mechanisms...

And we try to understand the scale at which all this is carried out, we either have epiphany, or we continue to not get it, numbed in disbelief. Numbed by our desire to only consider what we can rationalize.

Those who don't 'get it', become disassociated form the reality of the millions, choosing instead to associate with the reality of a few, yet ignorant to their own place in that number of MILLIONS.

Map

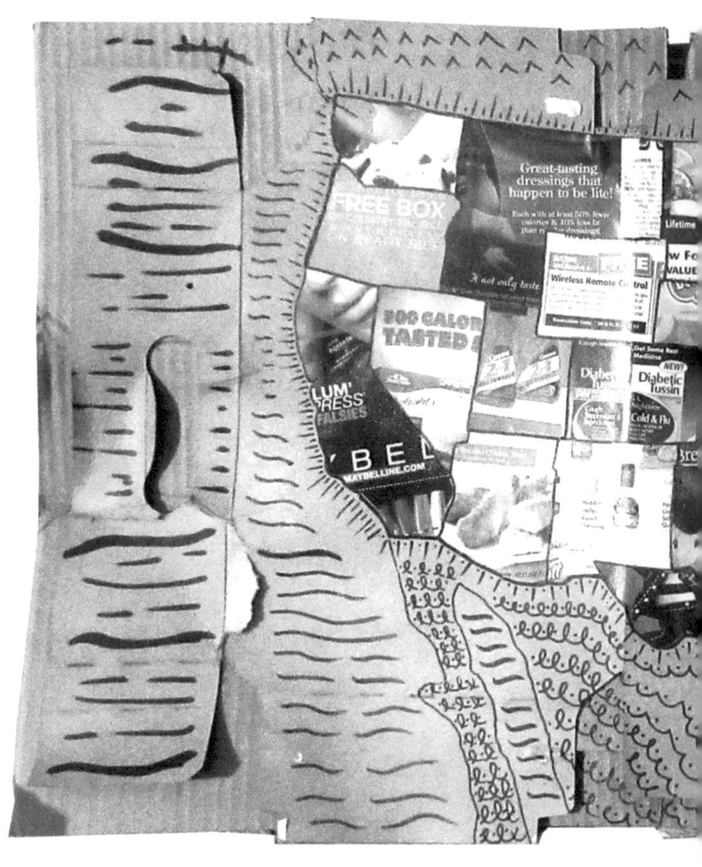

Cutout advertisements, acrylic, Ink, mixed
media on cardboard.
19 x 28" (Approx)
2012

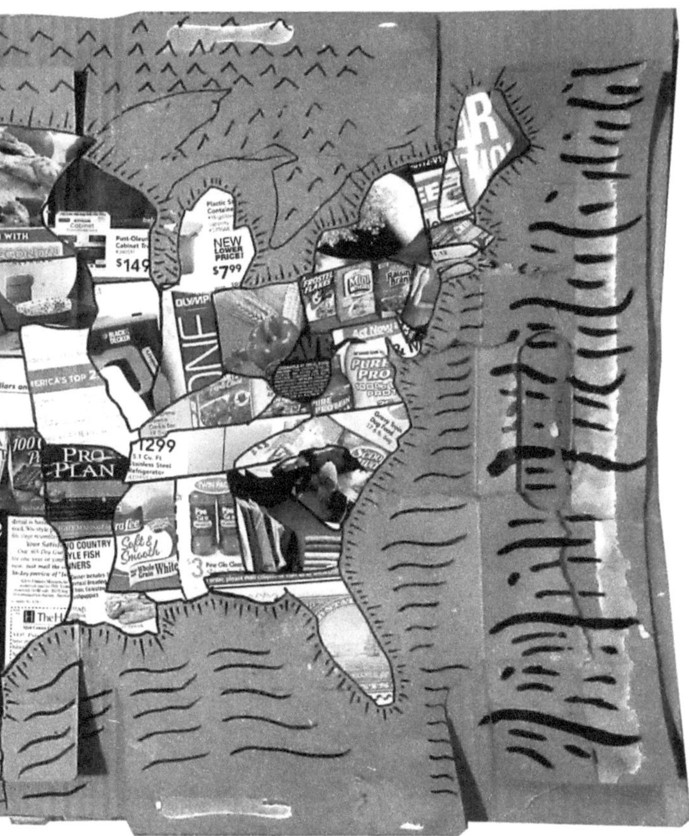
I WITH
$149
Cabinet
Rust-Oleum
Cabinet Tra
Plastic S
Containe
NEW
LOWER
PRICE!
$7 99
OLYMP
ONE
BLACK
DECKER
AMERICA'S TOP 2
llars america's top 2
100
PRO
PLAN
1299
5.1 Cu. Ft
Stainless Steel
Refrigerator
FROSTED
FLAKES
Mini
Raisin
Bran
Act Now!
PURE
PRO
PRO
PURE
PROTEIN
TWIN PAC
ra Lee
Soft &
Smooth
Whole
Grain White
3
Pre Glo Clea
R
O COUNTRY
YLE FISH
NERS
Your Satisf
The H

Pieces 'Millions'

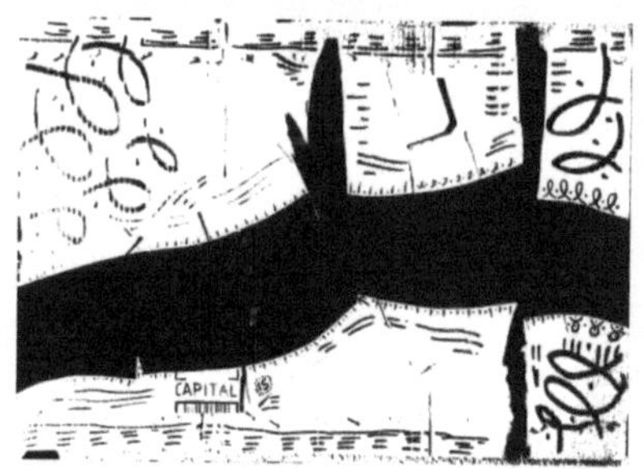

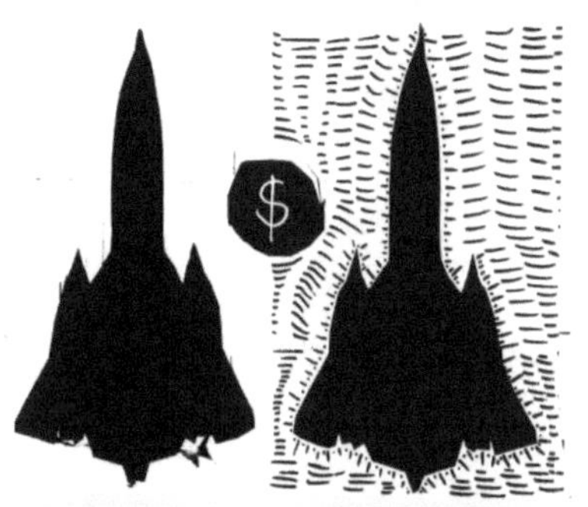

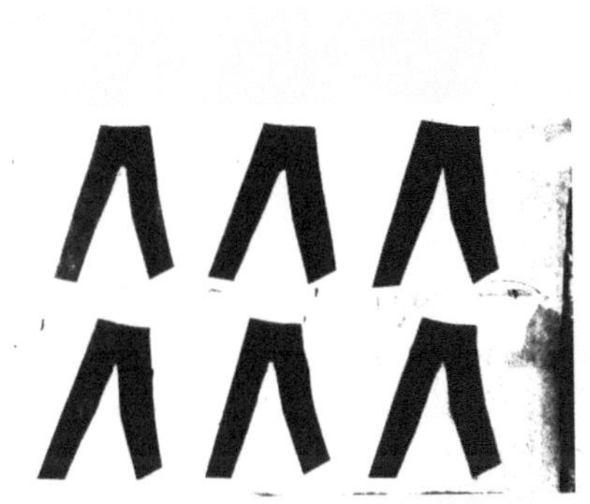

Pants.
Paper on cardboardl.
8 x 11" (Approx)
2012

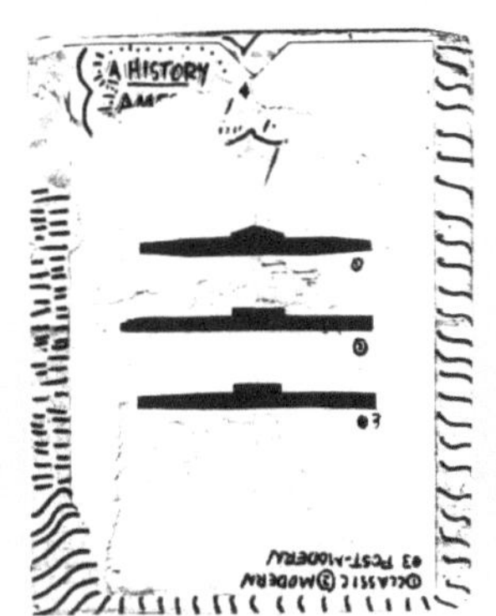

American
Architecture.
Paper, marker on
cardboardl.
4.5 x 7" (Approx)
2012

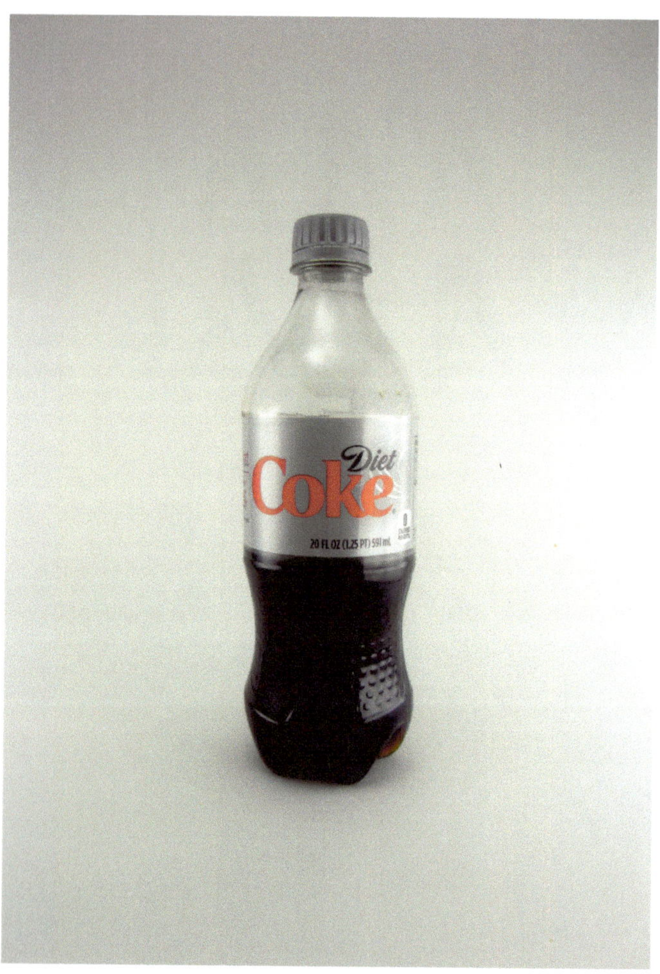

Diet
Coke
20 FL OZ (1.25 PT) 591 mL

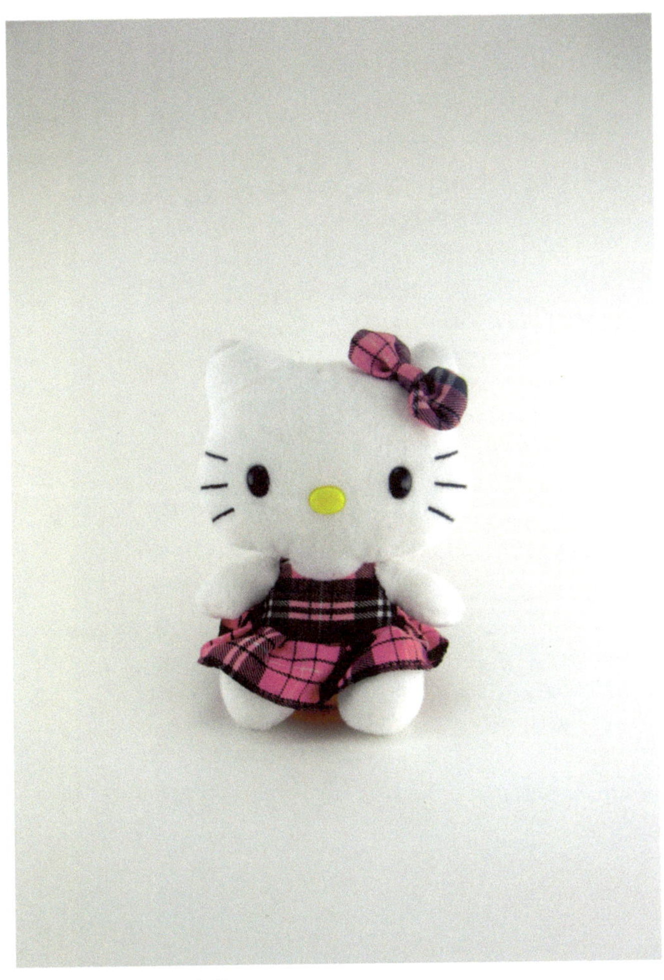

Iconography, 2 c-prints. 5x7".
2012

49

A SHIRT

DURING THE PRODUCTION PROCESS OF MILLIONS, I MADE SOME IMAGES INTO A SCREENPRINT. THIS WAS TO GIVE ME THE ABILITY TO SCREEN PRINT THE PANTS THAT HUNG IN THE BACK OF THE SHOW WITH THE "MILLIONS" CIRCLE.

I DECIDED TO MAKE A T-SHIRT FOR MYSELF TO WEAR WITH THAT LOGO. I WORE IT CONTINUOUSLY FOR A FEW MONTHS UNTIL THE SHOW WENT OVER TIME AND MY CAT STARTED RIPPING UP THE SHOULDERS. (HE LIKES TO RIDE AROUND ON MY SHOULDERS).

THE IDEA OF A UNIFORM, EVEN IF JUST A T-SHIRT ALLOWED ME TO FEEL PART OF THE CONTINUED VIEWING OF THE ART, A REMINDER THAT WHILE I MAY NOT BE MAKING A STATEMENT RIGHT NOW, MY ART IS ACTIVELY SENDING A MESSAGE TO FOLKS WHILE I'M SHOWING IT. ESSENTIALLY, I FORCED ME TO BE PRESENT WITH REALITY.

A Millions Shirt

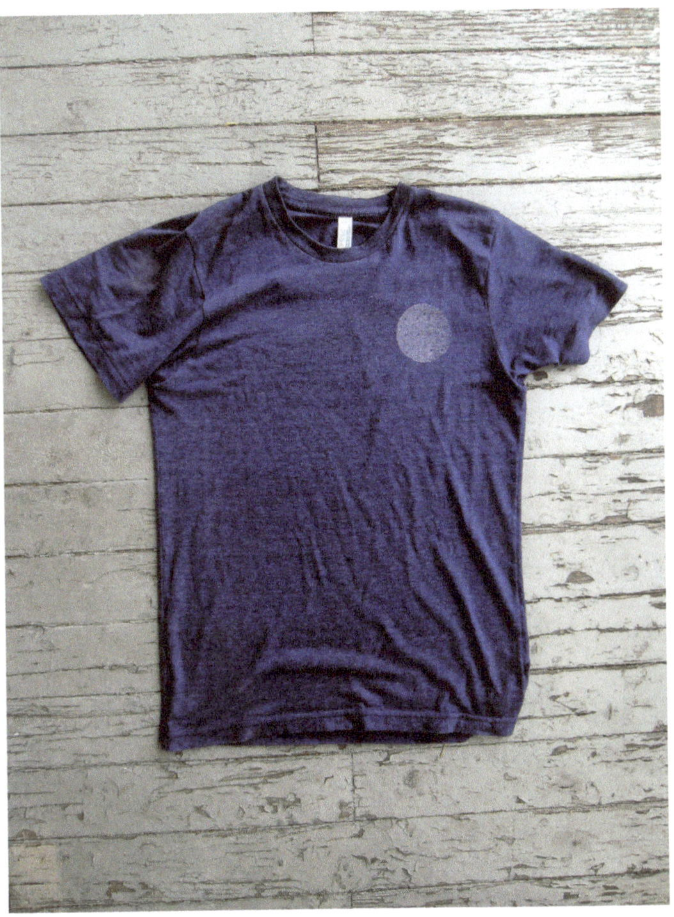

IT's IN OUR MIND

FOLLOWING THE "MILLIONS" SHOW, ANOTHER SHOW WAS ANNOUNCED...
"ON OUR FRONT DOOR STEP" WAS AN EXHIBITION OF ART REGARDING
THE INSTITUTIONALIZED NATURE OF VIOLENCE.

VIOLENCE IS A SUBJECT THAT INTERESTS ME GREATLY, AS
WE OFTEN TEND TO NOT REALIZE THE VIOLENCE WE EITHER
WITNESS OR PARTICIPATE DIRECTLY IN.
THIS SHOW WAS HELD BY THE GENDER STUDIES DEPt.
AT VCU. HERE IN RICHMOND, VIRGINIA.

FROM MY OWN EXPERIENCE WITH VIOLENCE, I KNOW
IT IS A MINDSET. A PATH WITH WHICH WE
REACT WITH VIOLENT OPTIONS. It IS A DICHOTOMY
WE FEEL INVOLVED IN. WE SEE FEW OTHER OPTIONS.
LEARNING THAT THE FALSE CHOICE OF VIOLENCE
IS ONLY A REALITY IN OUR MINDS IS THE
BREAKTHROUGH STEP TO LEARNING NOT TO HURT
THOSE AROUND US, EVEN WHILE IMMERSED IN
A CULTURE THAT IS TYPICALLY VIOLENT.

THE SHOW RAN FROM April 23 2012 - August 27th 2012.
THIS IS THE PIECE I SUBMITTED...

it's in
our mind

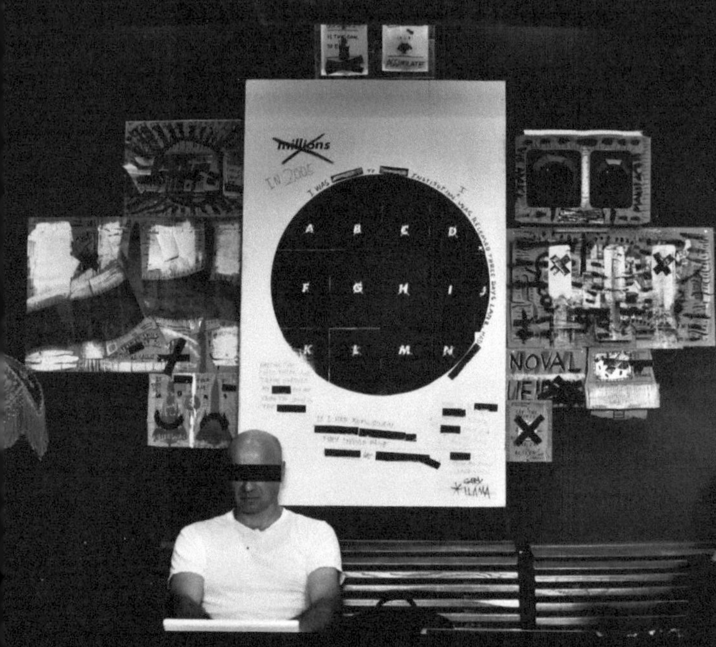

Millions (redacted)

May-August 2012.
Crossroads Coffee & Ice Cream
Richmond, Virginia

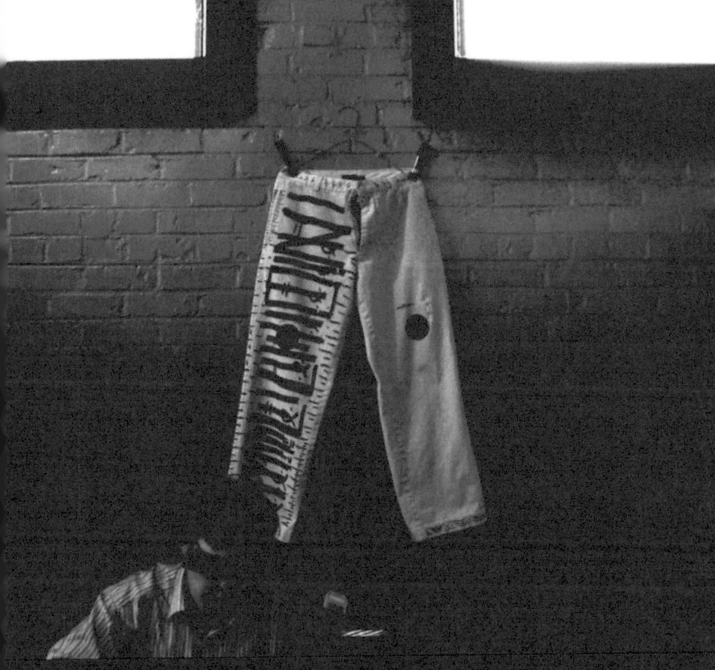

...the end of April, the business I had installed 'Millions' at informed me they had no upcoming shows, and I could put up new pieces, and keep the wall for another month or so...

...ad just been in an argument with a VCU psychiatry (or psychology) student, about whether ECT is effective. My spouse had recently been involved with the OCCUPY APA event. So Overall I had ...n cultivating a lot of compassion for those whom have dealt with the mental health industry, and in ...rticular, those who fell victim to the loosness in which it's diagnostic criteria is applied, usually not ...n in acordance with what the DSM-IV states as neccessary for diagnosis.

...wing studied a bit about the process, as well has having been personally involved in them as a ...tient, I realized that while the industry largely may try to be scientific, it's diagnoses largely on what ...not be ruled out as coincidence.

...nd accordingly, is something of a psuedoscience.

...nd it's a pseudoscience people subscribe to. Every patient puts themselves at risk of the wrong ...agnosis, at a level of incidence that is probably higher than we can imagine.

...very patient puts themselves as Guinea Pig, as lab rat, for one of a dozen drugs that MAY help a ...mptom, but although the doctors may know how the drug is sipposed to work, they have no idea why it ...orks or doesn't in a particular person, and not others.

...ntinued on page 61)

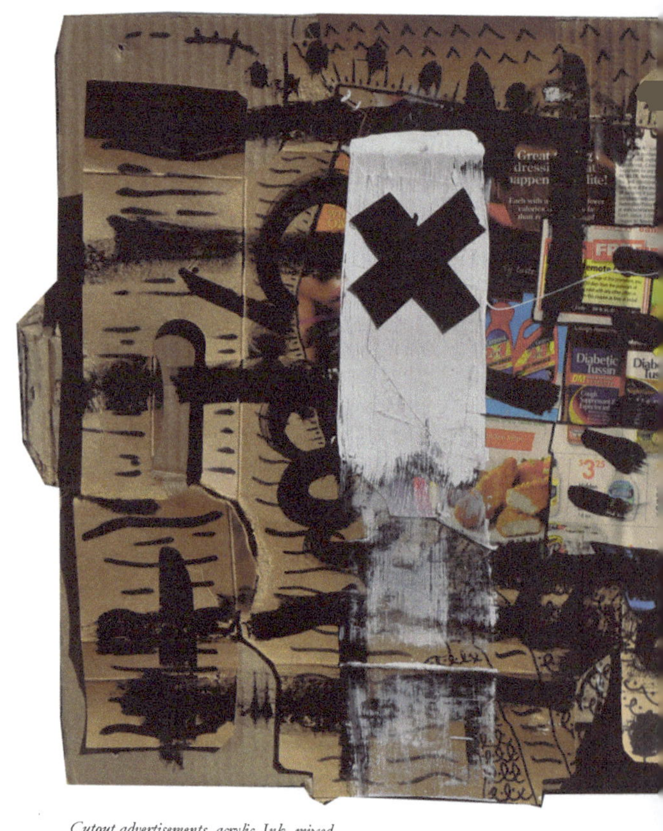

*Cutout advertisements, acrylic, Ink, mixed
media on cardboard.
19 x 28" (Approx)
2012*

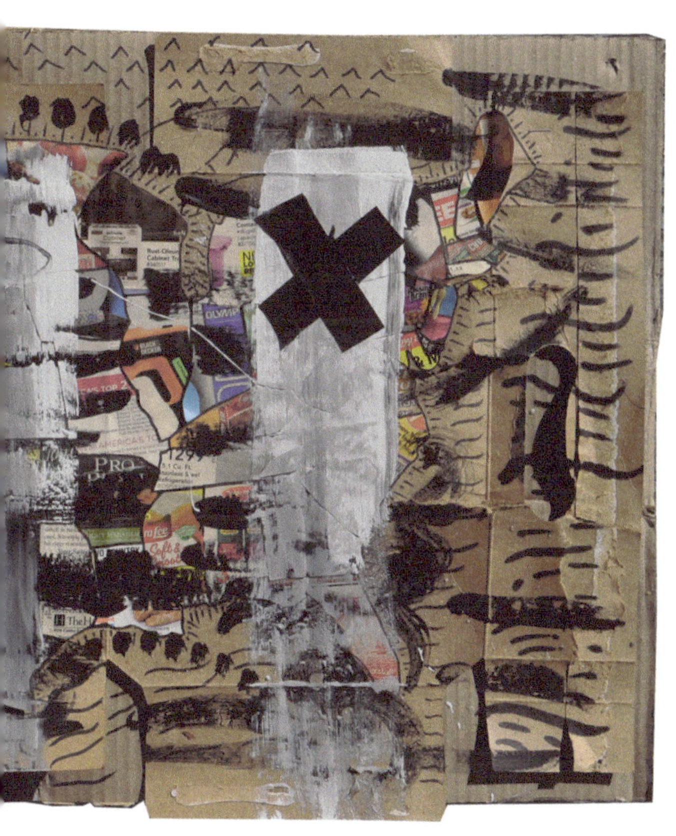

Pieces 'Millions (redacted)'

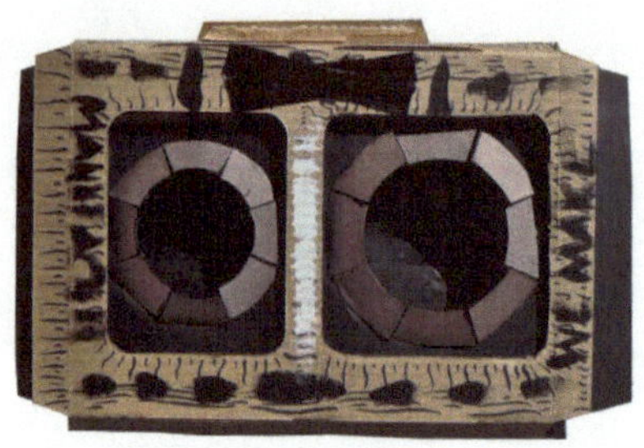

Capital Snake.
Acrylic, mixed
media on
cardboard.
11 x 18"
(Approx)
2012

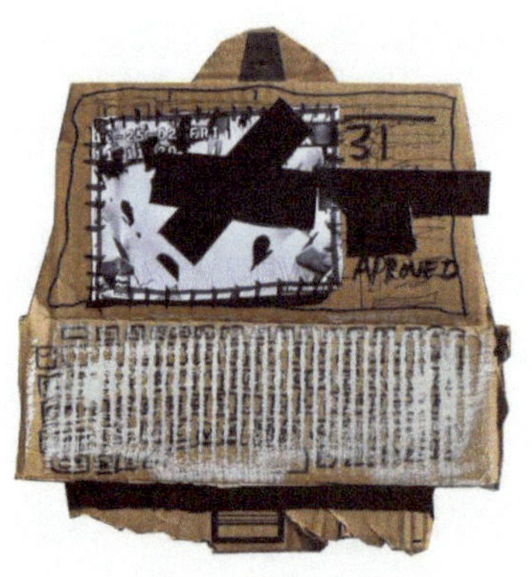

Capital Bird.
Paper on
cardboard.
8 x 14" (Approx)
2012

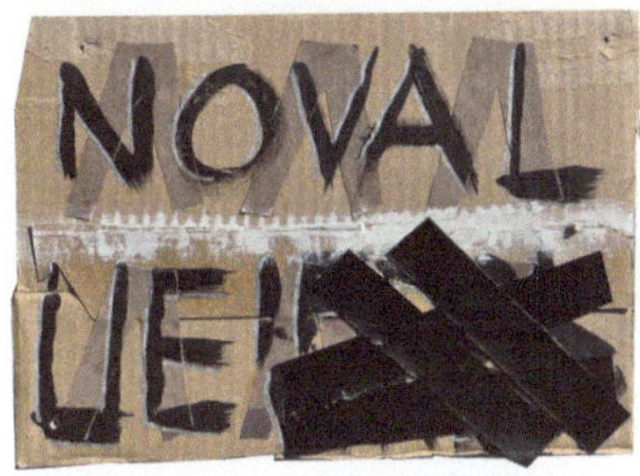

Pants.
Paper on cardboardl.
8 x 11" (Approx)
2012

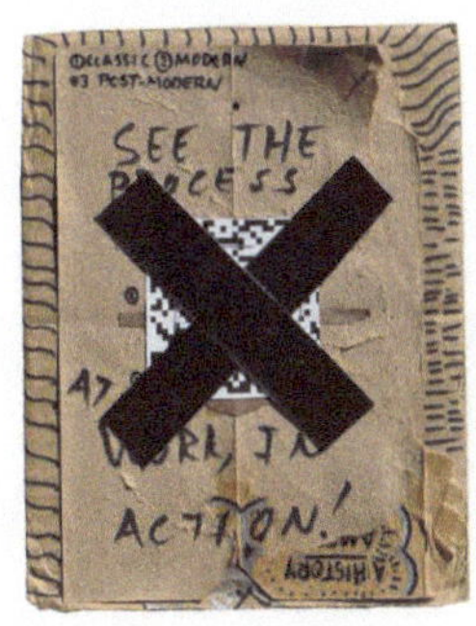

American
Architecture.
Paper, marker on
cardboardl.
4.5 x 7" (Approx)
2012

*Capital Snake.
Acrylic, mixed
media on
cardboard.
19 x 24"
(Approx)
2012*

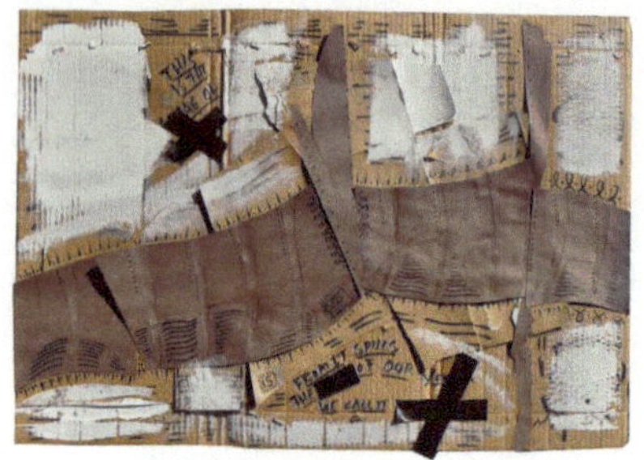

*Capital Bird.
Paper on
cardboard.
8 x 11" (Approx)
2012*

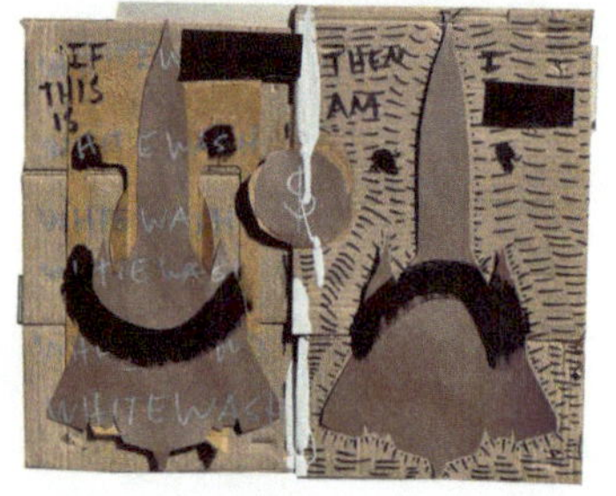

Pieces: Millions (redacted - Cont)

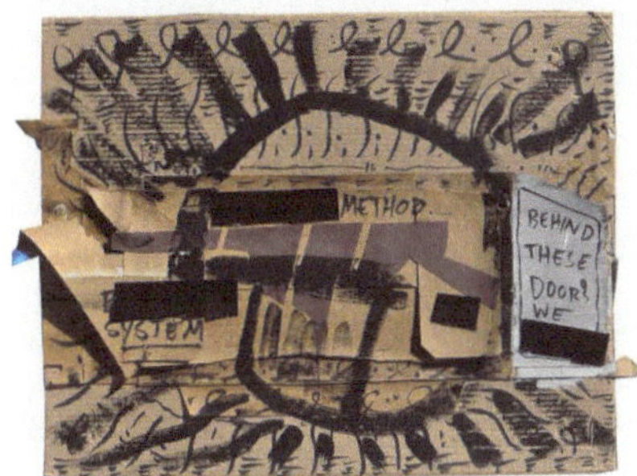

Pants.
Paper on cardboardl.
8 x 11" (Approx)
2012

The saddest part is, for folks in crisis, this is the best we can do currently.
If I had to come up with a solution to all of this, I would say, make the
experimental nature of these drugs and procedures know. Make the reality
of diagnosis as a realtive function of the diagnoser known. Know that
finding a good doctor you can trust is the big thing standing between effective
treatment and a nightmare experience. And that such a doctor can only
guaranetee so much succes, considering the critera and lack of knowledge
about the human psyche. And above all, talk to other folks like yourself
about issues like this. Compassion is the anti-dote to dehumanization.

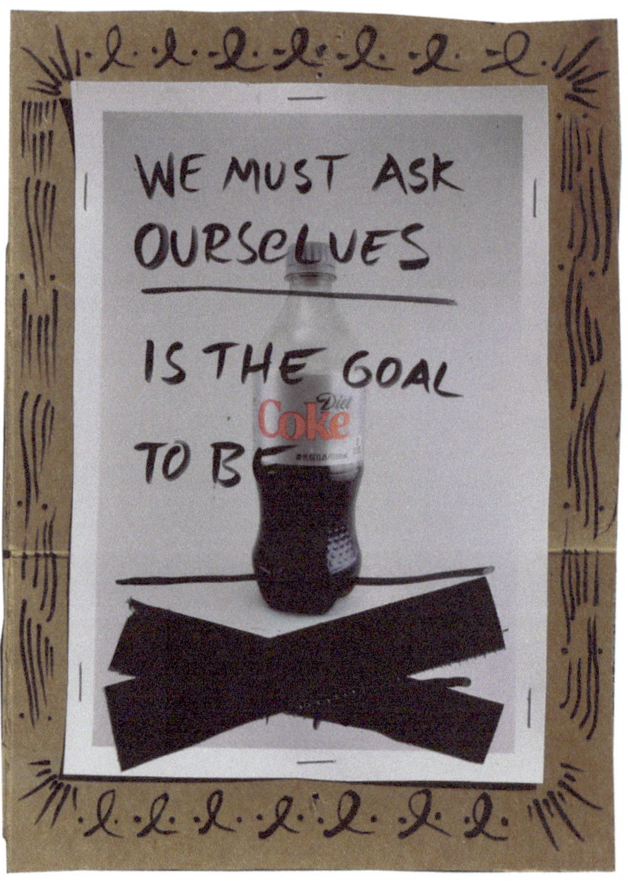
WE MUST ASK
OURSELVES

IS THE GOAL
TO BE
Diet Coke

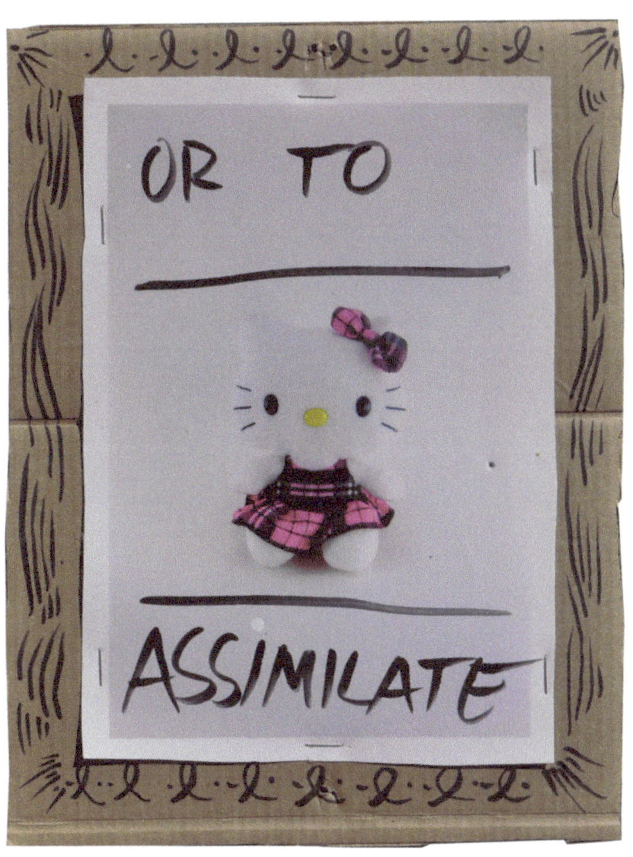

Iconography, 2 c-prints. 5x7".
2012

Etagere.
Wood, Metal,
Acrylic.
24 x 54 x 11".
2012

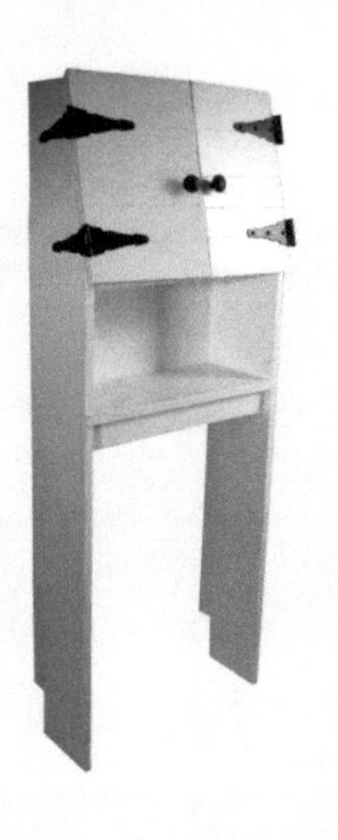

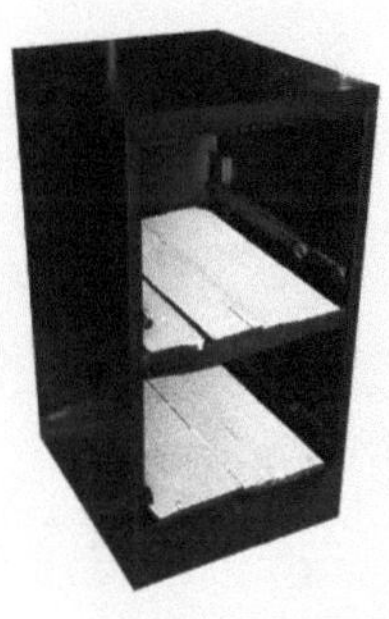

Filing Cabinet.
Metal, wood, acrylic.
14 × 28 × 18".
2013

Few.
Print on paper,
staples.
8.5 x 33".
2013

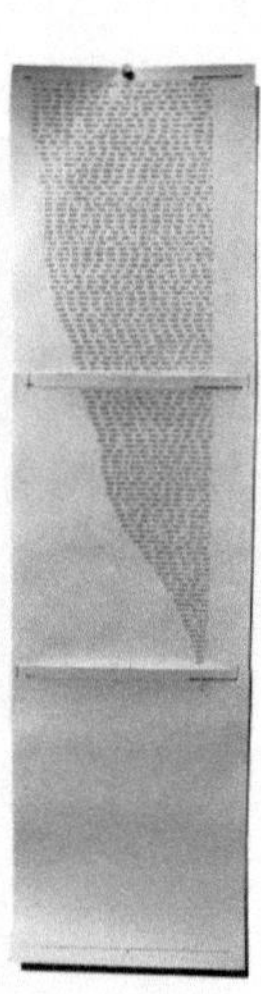

Pieces: Wild Birds

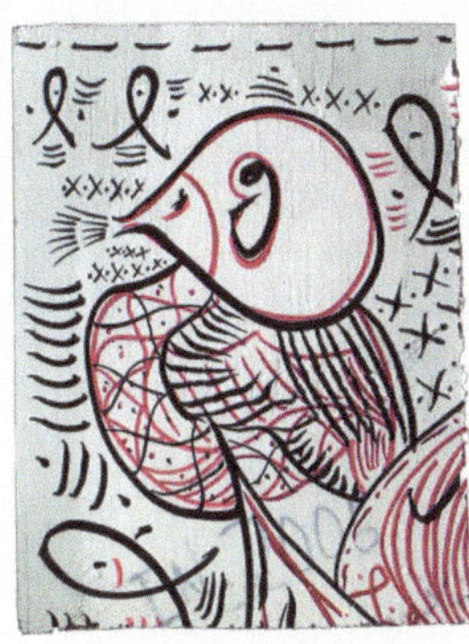

fig. 1
Acrylic on wood.
11 x 15" (Approx)
2013

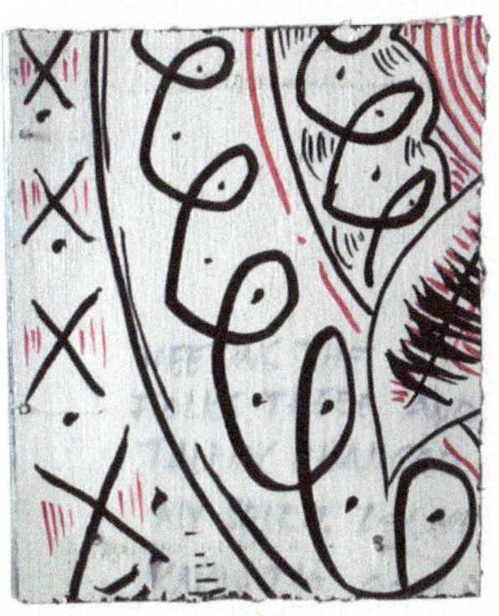

fig. 2
Acrylic on wood.
11 x 15" (Approx)
2013

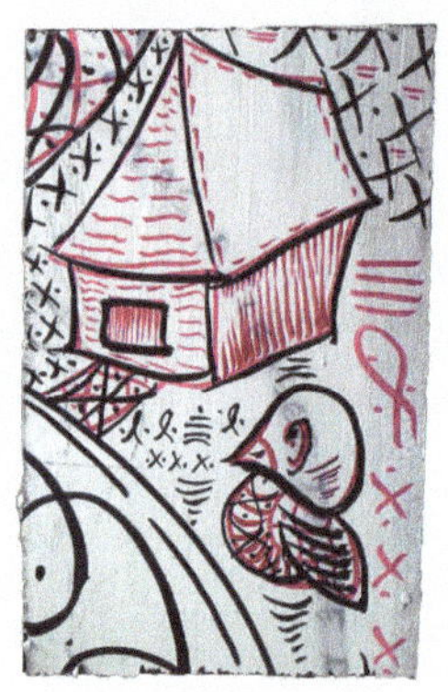

fig. 3
Acrylic on wood.
11 x 15"
(Approx)
2013

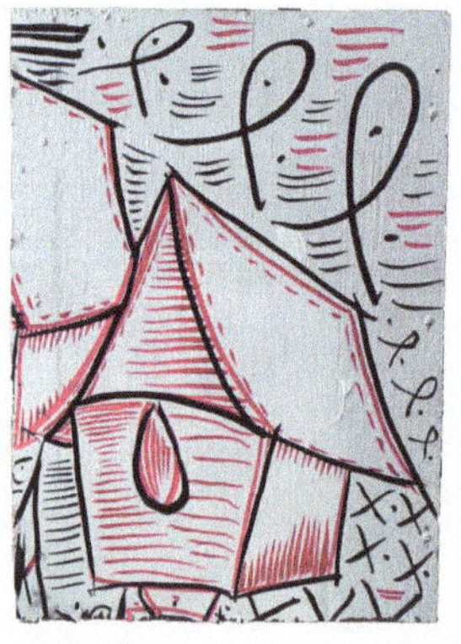

fig. 4
Acrylic on wood.
11 x 15"
(Approx)
2013

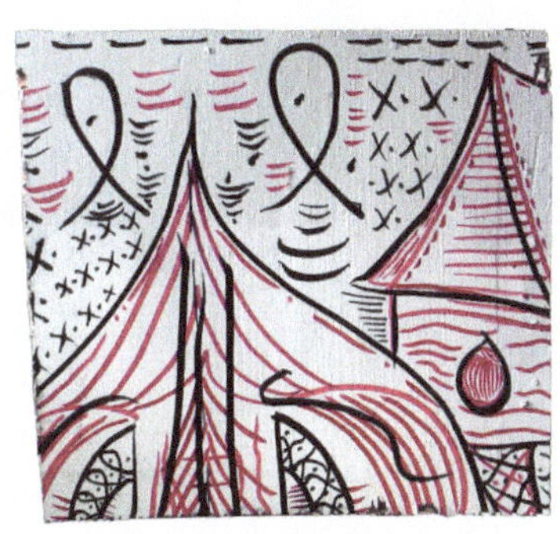

fig. 5
Acrylic on wood.
11 x 15" (Approx)
2013

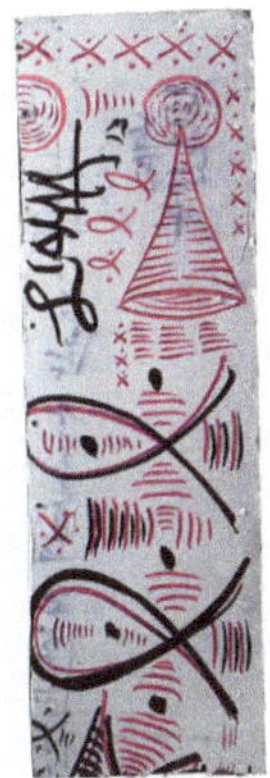

fig. 6
Acrylic on wood.
11 x 28" (Approx)
2013

Pieces Birds

fig. 1
Ink on paper.
9 x 13" (Approx)
2013

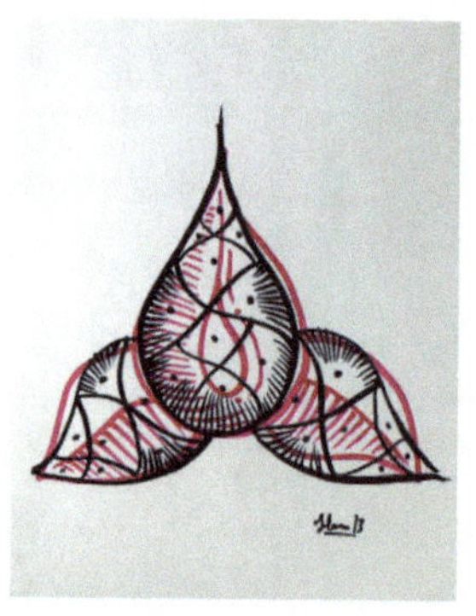

fig. 2
Ink on paper.
9 x 13" (Approx)
2013

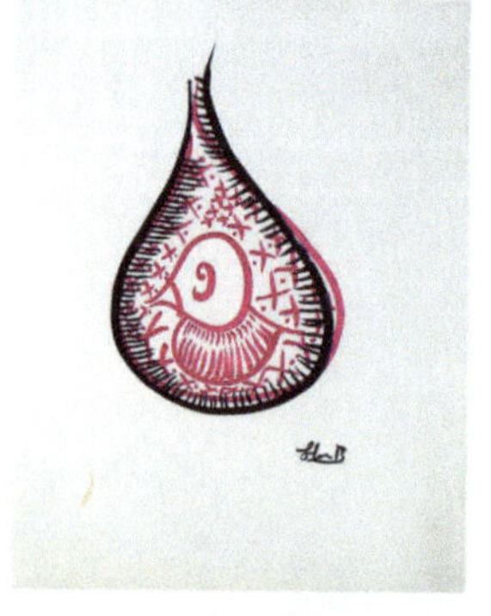

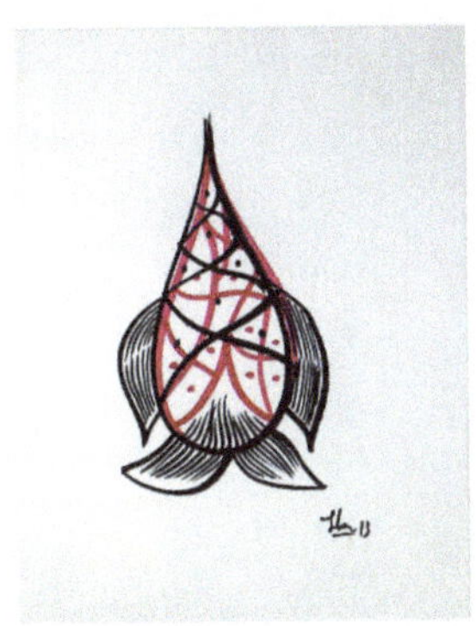

fig. 3
Ink on paper.
9 x 13" (Approx)
2013

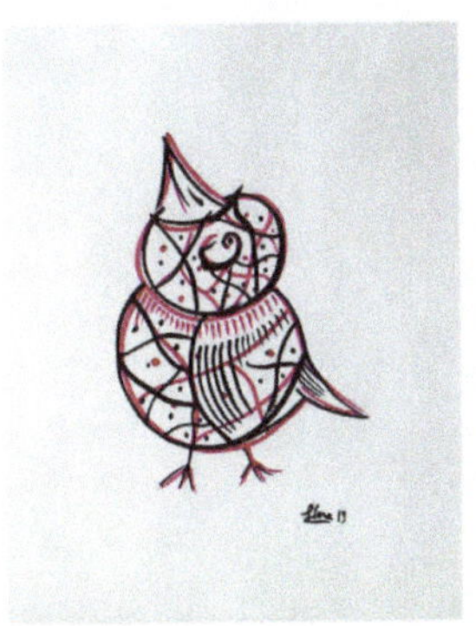

fig. 4
Ink on paper.
9 x 13" (Approx)
2013

fig. 5
Ink on paper.
9 x 13" (Approx)
2013

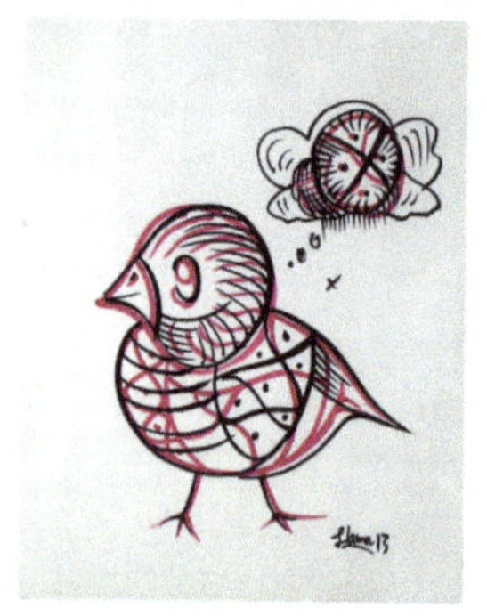

fig. 6
Ink on paper.
9 x 13" (Approx)
2013

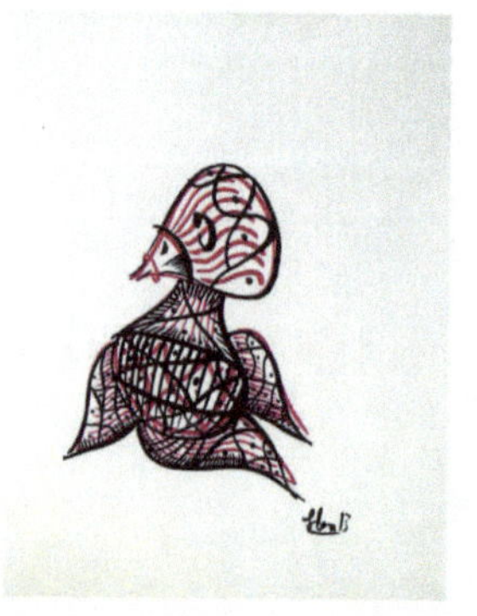

Pieces: Birds (cont)

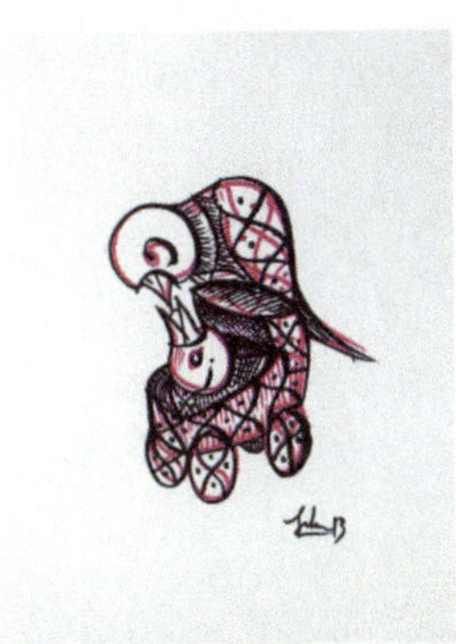

fig. 7
Ink on paper.
9 x 13" (Approx)
2013

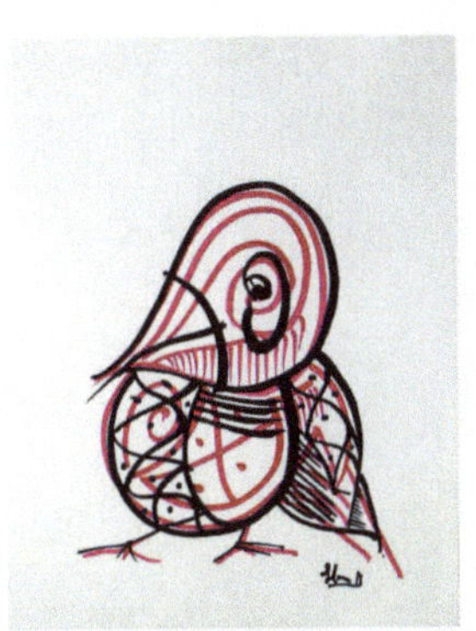

fig. 8
Ink on paper.
9 x 13" (Approx)
2013

fig. 9
Ink on paper.
9 x 13" (Approx)
2013

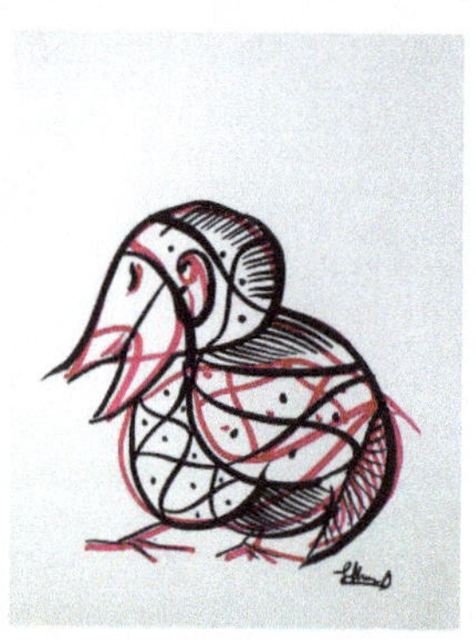

Pieces: Birdhouses

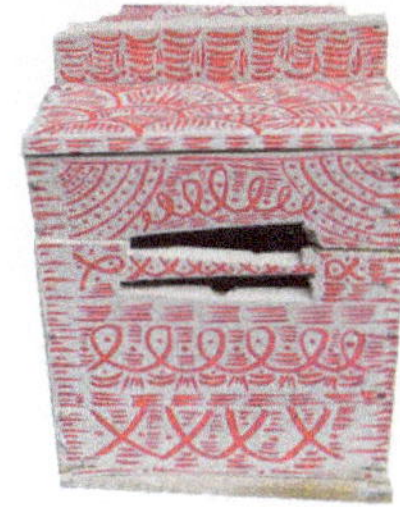

fig. 1
*Ink, acrylic, glue on
woodr.
9 x 13" x 4 (Approx)
2013*

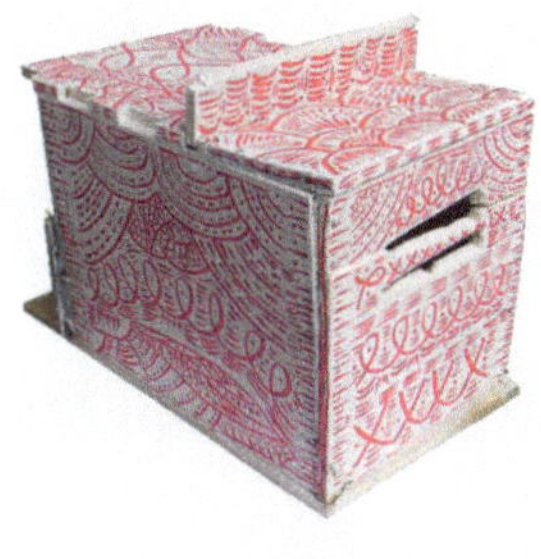

Pieces Birdhouses

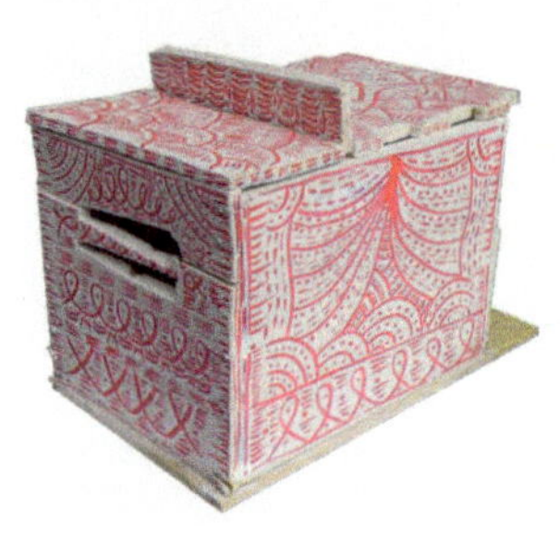

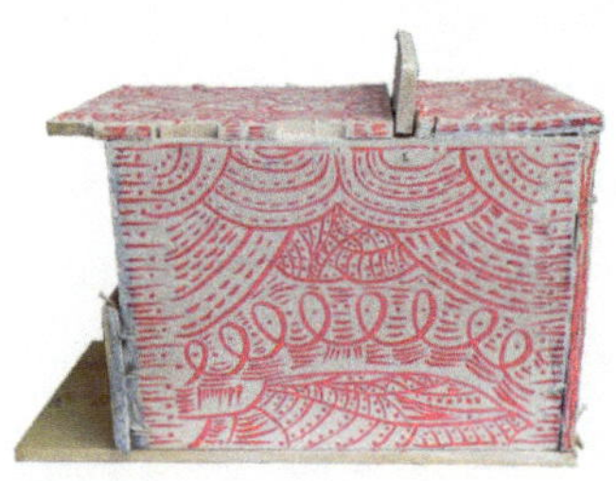

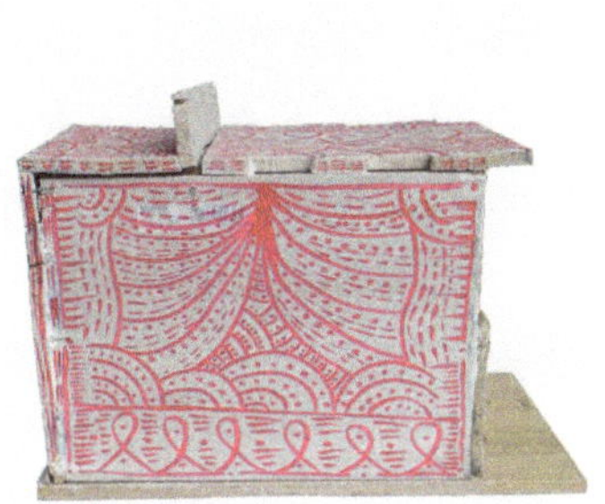

fig. 2
Ink, acrylic, glue on
woodr.
9 x 11" x 3
(Approx)
2013

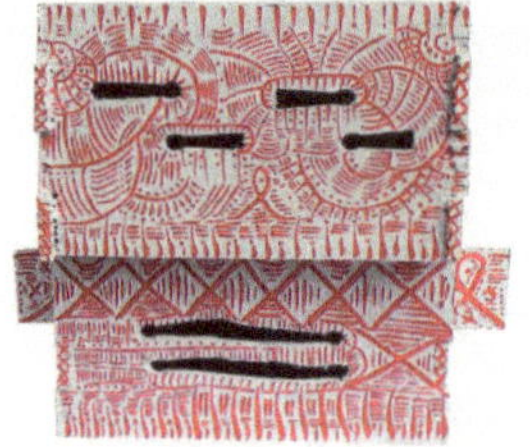

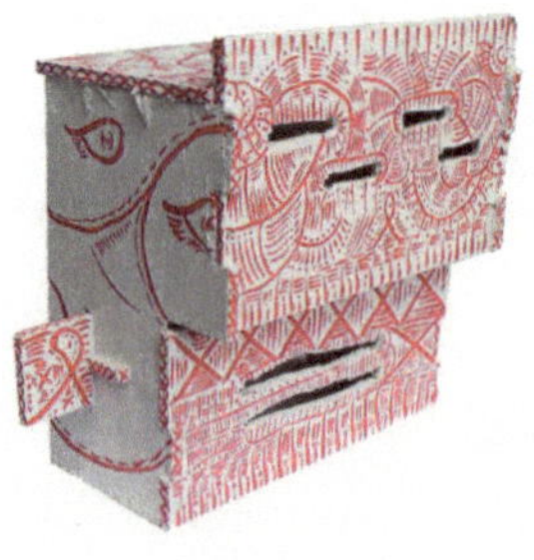

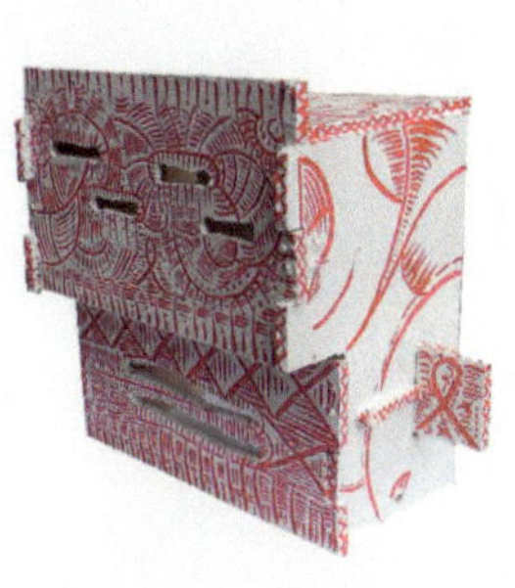

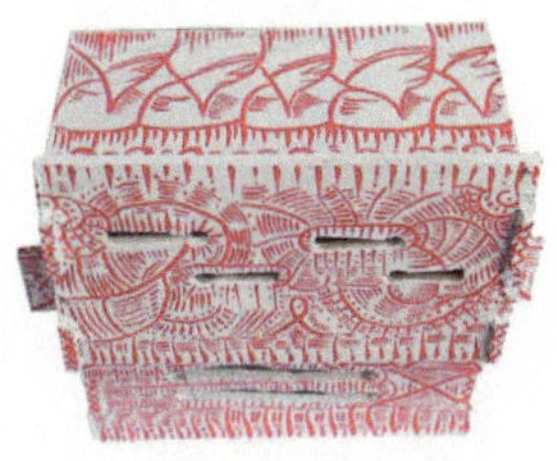

fig. 3
Ink, acrylic, glue on
woodr.
6 x 11" x 4
(Approx)
2013

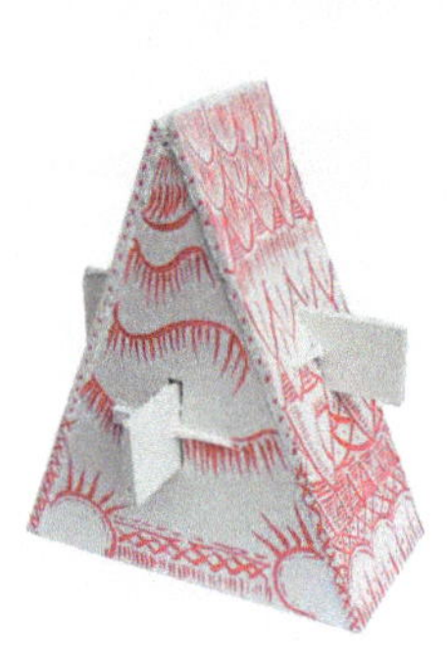

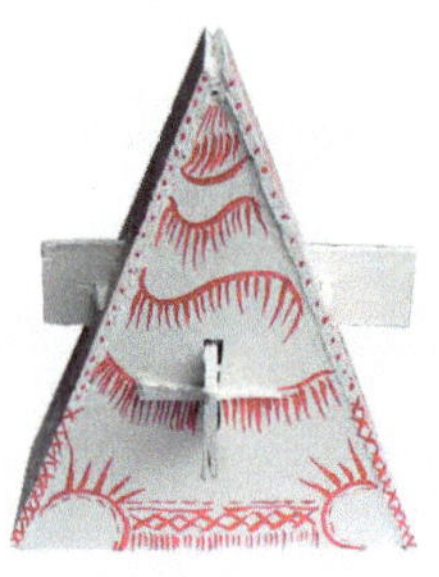

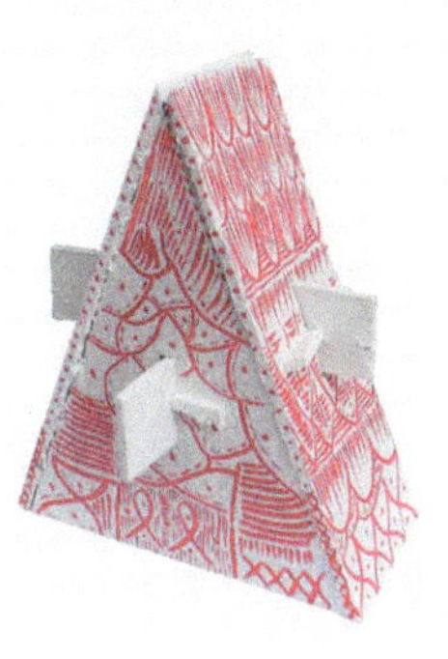

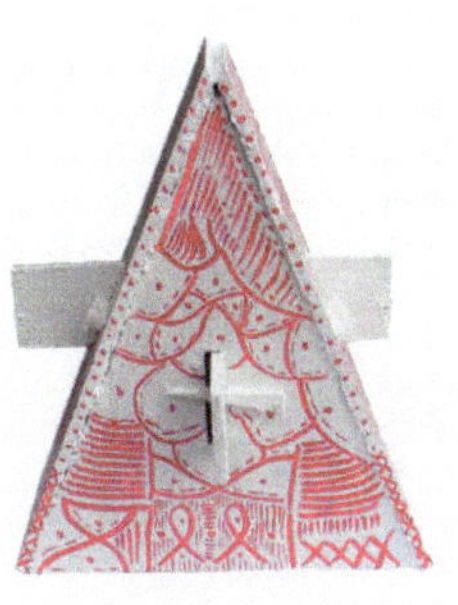

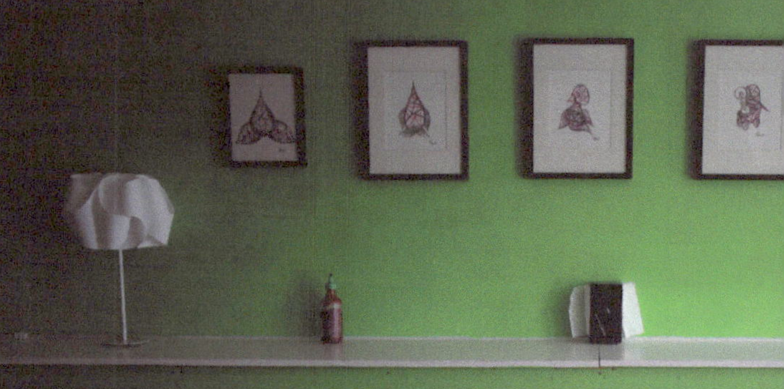

A Life Cycle Of Wild Birds

March 2014.
Cafe Verde
Richmond, Virginia

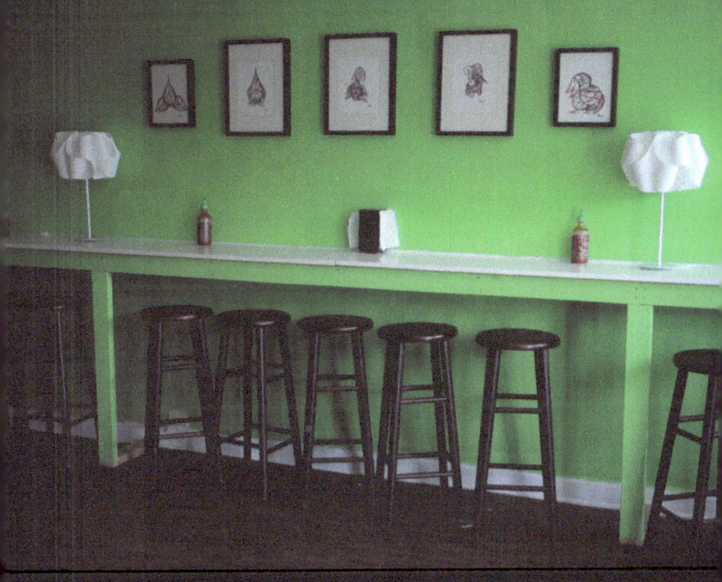

In 2014, I put up this exhibition of some pieces from my 'Wild Birds' works. Initially, I was planning to install everything from my Birds works: Birdhouses, Panels, Painting and drawings, but found out near the last minute that the space only wanted a few pieces.

So I went through the drawings and came up with these five images, which showed the progression of the bird from conception to old age.

There is something about using the form of a bird to show emotion that I find to humanize the emotions to the viewer.

Odd.

Pieces Little Friends

fig. 1
Acrylic on wood.
3 x 4 (Approx)
2014

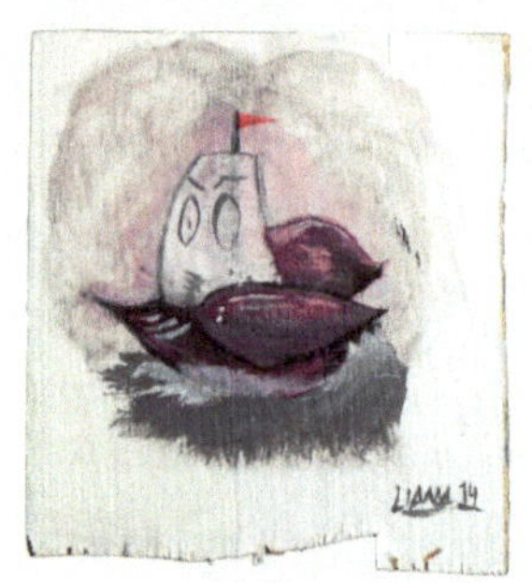

fig. 2
Acrylic on wood.
3 x 4 (Approx)
2014

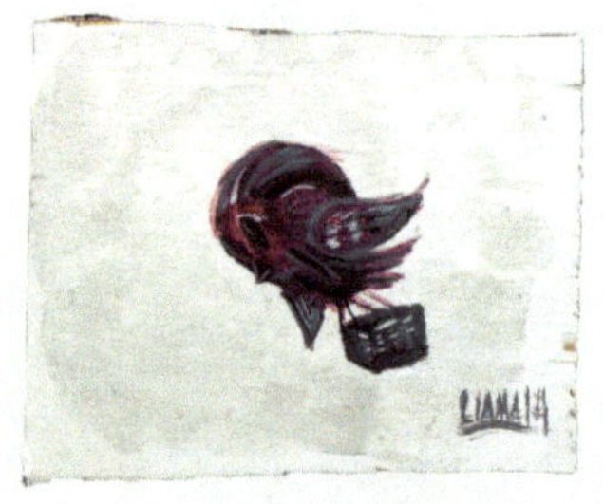

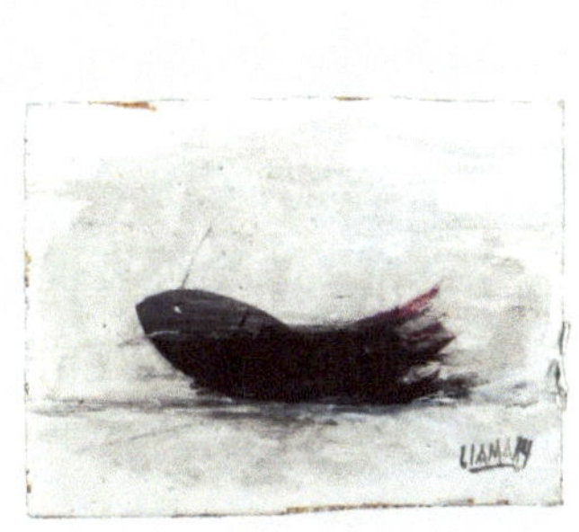

fig. 3
Acrylic on wood.
3 x 4 (Approx)
2014

Pieces Tears

fig. 1
Acrylic on wood.
3 x 4 (Approx)
2014

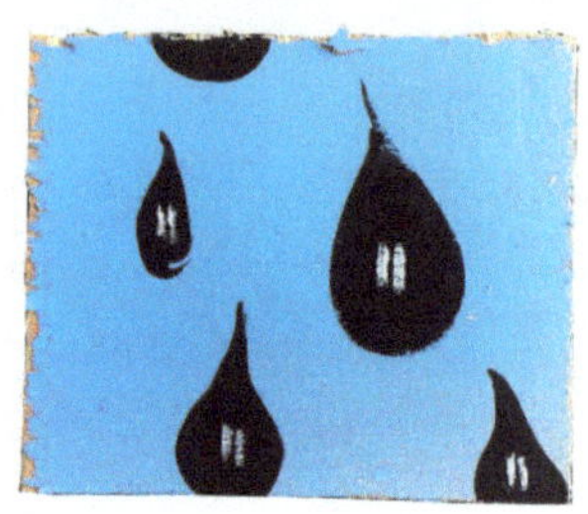

fig. 2
Acrylic on wood.
3 x 4 (Approx)
2014

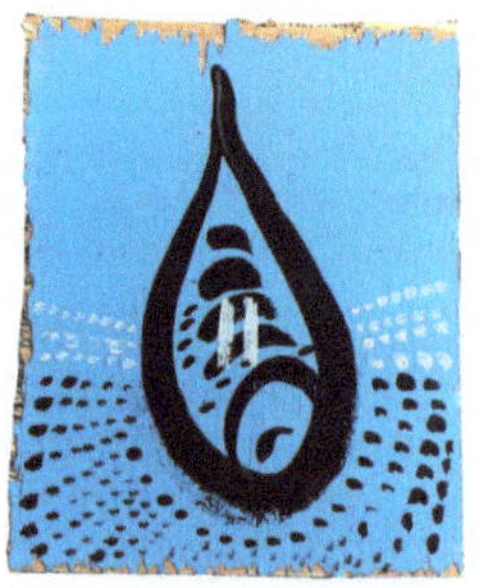

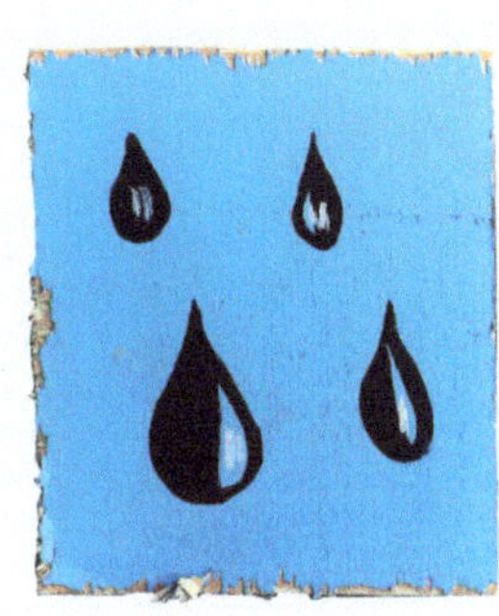

fig. 3
Acrylic on wood.
3 x 4 (Approx)
2014

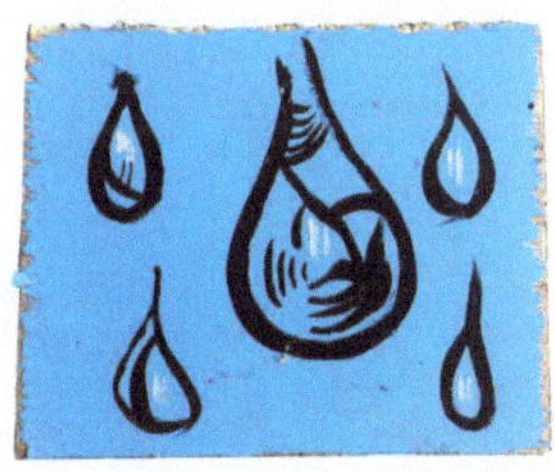

fig. 4
Acrylic on wood.
3 x 4 (Approx)
2014

fig. 5
Acrylic on wood.
3 x 4 (Approx)
2014

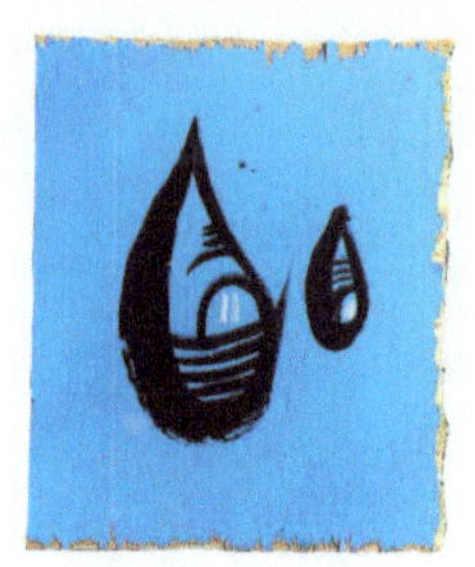

fig. 6
Acrylic on wood.
3 x 4 (Approx)
2014

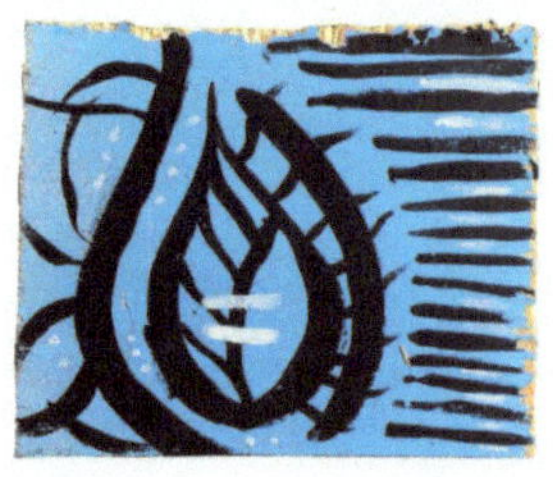

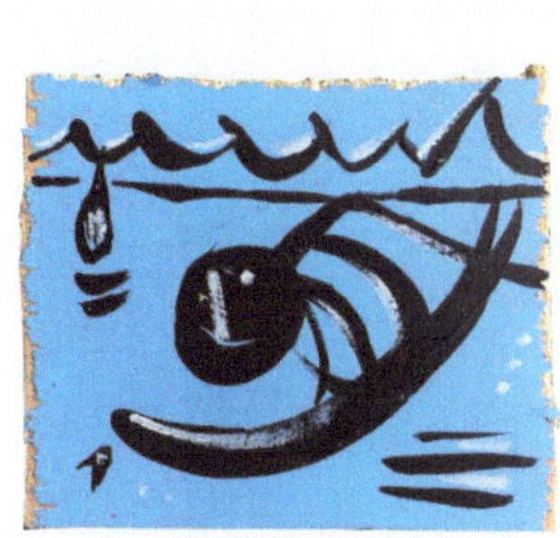

fig. 7
Acrylic on wood.
3 x 4 (Approx)
2014

Goose

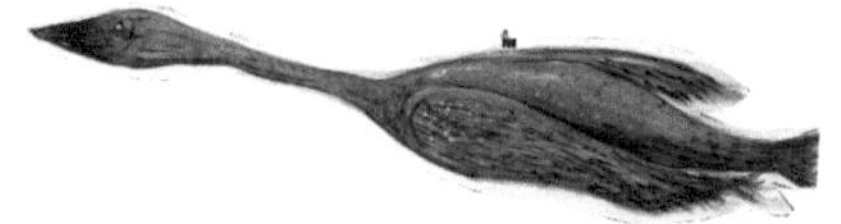

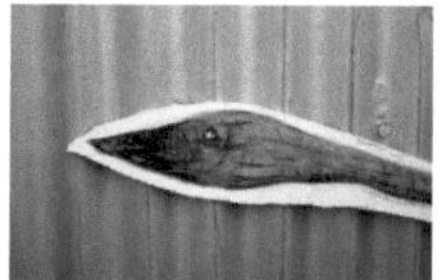

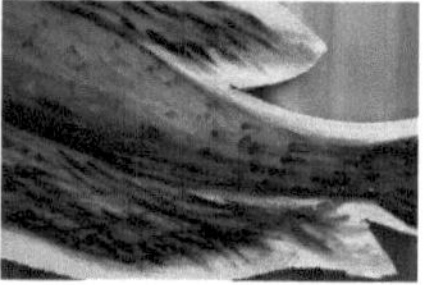

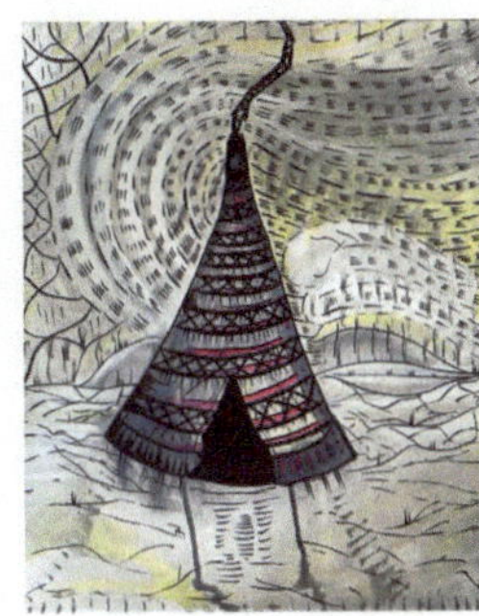

fig. 1
Acrylic on canvas.
18 x 21" (Approx)
2015

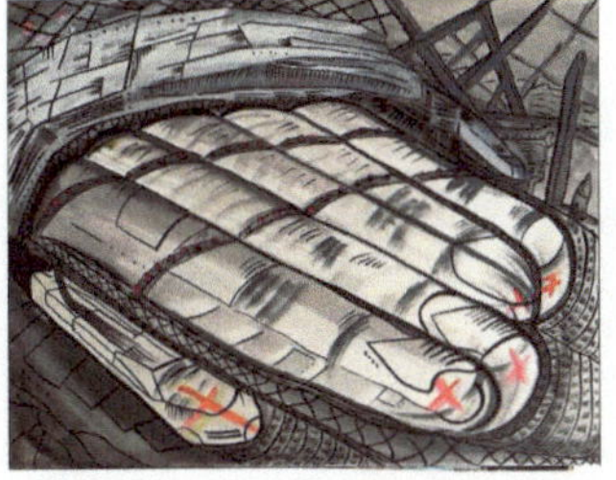

fig. 2
Acrylic on canvas.
18 x 21" (Approx)
2015

www.ingramcontent.com/pod-product-compliance
Lightning Source LLC
Chambersburg PA
CBHW041231050726
47599CB00007B/906